An Introduction to the

Art & Science

of

Johannes Liechtenauer's

Medieval German

Longsword

by Chris Stride

Printed in Great Britain

ISBN 978-0-9564871-1-7

Edited by
Barbara Shellard M.A. (Oxon.), M.Litt.

Published by Wyvern Media Ltd
United Kingdom
www.wyvernmedia.co.uk

Design, layout and cover: James Payton

An introduction to an interpretation of

German Medieval Longsword

As set down by

Johannes Liechtenauer

(in circa 1370)

Glossed by

Sigmund Ringeck

(circa 1508)

Equally humbly expanded here in this little book by

Chris Stride

(circa 2011)

A manual concerning Longsword Grades 1 & 2

"Young knight, learn to love God and to respect women, so shall your honour grow"

(Liechtenauer)

Written by Chris Stride

A further expansion to the original text of Sigmund Ringeck the Elder by Chris Stride

Interpretation of the manuscript by Chris Stride and P. Willaume

From Master Ringeck's manual dated between 1502–1508, as translated in this instance by Dr R.E.Kellett

Acknowledgements

The time I have spent practising and teaching HEMA has been a journey of discovery from the beginning and I am far from being at the end of the adventure even now, but along the path travelled so far I have made many valuable and close friends to whom I am indebted. I must start at the beginning and thank Philippe Willaume for introducing me to Ringeck, and consequently Liechtenauer. The 10 years or so that Philippe and I spent getting our collective teeth into German longsword, and trying to kill one another with swords as a consequence, brought light and clarity to both our understanding of, and respect for, the Art. I also owe a debt of thanks to Herbert Schmidt for his interest in this interpretation and for challenging my understanding, thus forcing me to consider and reconsider what I know, combined with his constant nagging for me to get it into print. I must thank Jonathan Miller for his support from our first meeting and for his persistence in getting me involved with the British Federation for Historical Swordplay, and Dr Rachel Kellett for her patience and dedication towards accurately translating the Ringeck script for me and putting up with my queries and requests. I owe a debt of gratitude to Mark Hillyard for his knowledge of all things chivalrous, his unique vision and ever-persistent desire to see me, as with many others, commit research to print; to Mark Lancaster for his constant enthusiasm, vast knowledge, understanding and never-failing enthusiasm for all things medieval longsword-related, as well as for offering to publish this book; to Barry and Kim Young for their unique approach to life and for forcing me to think even further 'outside the box' with their 'Italian ways'; to Dave Casserly for his support and encouragement; and to Adrian Boyd, whose superior fitness and martial skills have always kept me grounded.

On a separate note, there are those outside the HEMA world who have been fundamental to the journey so far and to whom also I owe a debt of gratitude. Thanks must go to Chris Payne and Mike Portlock, respectively, whose friendship, generosity and use of facilities goes well beyond that of average friends; to Brigitte Daniel, for her amazing drawings that you find within the pages of this manual, combined with her generosity, support and encouragement throughout; to Barbara Shellard, for her devoted friendship, encouragement and editing skills; to Paul Binns, whose swordsmithing skills and depth of knowledge both of the history of swordsmithing and of metallurgy never cease to interest me; and to my students for believing that what I'm teaching has some value in their lives. Thank you to you all

Special thanks go to my parents, and especially to my Mother, who, from an early age, laid the foundation stones for this journey to be possible.

Mum, I dedicate this book to you.

Table of Contents

Introduction

This manual reflects the First and Second Grades as set out in the syllabus designed by Philippe Willaume and Christopher Stride and used by the School of Traditional Medieval Fencing. This syllabus was created around the **Fechtbuch** of Master Sigmund Ringeck the Elder, who wrote his Fechtbuch when, "...fencing master to his most noble Highness Albrecht, Count Palatine of the Rhine and Duke of Bavaria...". (The only time, to my knowledge, that an Albrecht was both Count Palatine of the Rhine and Duke of Bavaria is between 1502 and 1508, therefore it is reasonable to assume that this is very probably when his book was written.) Ringeck's Fechtbuch reflects the teachings of the great Master Johannes Liechtenauer who was teaching his system in the mid to late 14th Century and whose traditions, as far as we know, were passed down orally to his students, as there is currently no surviving documentation of the Liechtenauer verse outside that of his students' later work. Early references to Liechtenauer's verse are included in the writings of MS 3227a (otherwise known as Hanko Döbringer, c.1389) and Paulus Kal (c.1470).

There are a total of 6 grades within the syllabus concerning longsword and they reflect the information contained within the Ringeck Fechtbuch. Grades 1 & 2 lay the foundation for successive grades to build upon and the order in which the information is presented does not necessarily follow that found in the Ringeck book. The information has been slightly rearranged so that a balance of theory and practice is presented to the student in a logical and progressive manner. Not to absorb first and understand the information contained within this book before moving onto higher grades is a huge mistake, as the content is fundamental to the full understanding of the system and not just to that of the longsword discipline.

At no point is the information contained within this manual intended to be a definitive 'how to' guide to medieval German longsword but it is intended to provide a commentary on the interpretation and lessons as taught at the School. The reader will find within it basic martial principles and concepts that are true of any art, and a significant amount of material pertaining to the correct application of this particular martial discipline. Not only will this manual allow the student an opportunity to discover the system from the very core source, but also to understand the progressive nature and development of the Liechtenauer method, through Ringeck, to the present day. The content will be relevant for the novice and the more experienced student alike, and will have the intention of forming a proper basic foundation of understanding, the principles from which any martial system can be applied.

The format used by Ringeck to present his interpretation of the proper execution of the Liechtenauer method was to offer the Liechtenauer verse, then gloss the verse with an explanation. The manual will continue this tradition by using the Liechtenauer verse and Ringeck gloss as presented in the Ringeck manual, translated from Middle High German by Dr R.E.Kellett, a well-respected expert in Medieval German literature. It will provide you with a translation of the Liechtenauer text in *italics* and the Ringeck gloss. Where appropriate, there is a Stride 'Expansion' to explain further the intricacies of application regarding the attributes of a technique. When introducing an important element not covered in the original Liechtenauer text, or glossed upon by Ringeck, there is also the Stride 'Addition', the introduction to which is in the form of rhyming couplets to aid memory. This is in keeping with the spirit of the original Liechtenauer method. The 'Addition' could be used as a lesson and is not specifically related to the original Ringeck text but will provide the reader with some important principles which, if not already known, should dramatically improve the practitioner's understanding of the correct application of the Art.

Also presented is a very brief overview of medieval society, in an endeavour to compare the cultural differences between then and now. It is important to understand the mentality and moral obligations of the 14th Century Europeans, both socially and spiritually, in order to place the system into perspective relative to today. The intention behind the application of the system very much reflects these cultural elements, and to apply modern values to a discipline evolved from a bygone era without first understanding the mindset and moral convictions of that era is fundamentally flawed. A more in-depth examination of this subject will be discussed in future publications, building up a rounded picture of medieval hierarchical, spiritual and social culture.

No amount of text can replace the dedication and hard work required in mastering any art, be it martial or otherwise. Without this commitment to the art, the best any practitioner can expect is a mediocre understanding and poor execution of what can only be considered a way of life. Sacrifices have to be expected and time made available for many hours of practice in order to master any discipline. Some practitioners will find the physical co-ordination easier than others, and others may understand the principles better. Whatever the individual's strengths and weaknesses, it is necessary to be aware that the information provided in this manual will never replace the dedication necessary to master this, or any other, art. To this end, there is included a space after each technique for the students to make notes upon their observations, so improving their understanding and thus adding colour to their Art.

This interpretation of the Ringeck manuscript has been a result of more than 40 years of combined sword fighting and martial arts experience applied to the research and understanding of **HEMA** by Stride and Willaume, over 20 of which have been dedicated to Liechtenauer and specifically Ringeck. Although the content of this manuscript represents the author's current thinking on the system, it is likely that, as the process of research continues, this understanding will become more refined and an additional publication may be written to complement it. At no time will the fundamental principles change, so any future publication will become an addition to rather than a replacement of this one.

Medieval life, then and now....
(a brief overview)

Today our lives are very different from those of the late medieval period, and practitioners then would usually have come from the more privileged social backgrounds. For a knight, or mercenary, to become such, his training regarding the arts would have been his way of life from an early age, and he would most likely start his career from as young as 7 years. In order to remove the possibility of favour, and prepare the young boy for the independence of adulthood, he would be removed from his parental home and taken into the service of a wealthy relative, ideally of greater nobility than that of his parents, thus potentially promoting his social position. Being given the title of Page to his host, in exchange for menial duties the boy would learn the courtly arts vital for social progress (probably including some familiarity with contemporary and Classical poetry, history, etc.). Horsemanship, physical fitness and co-ordination would improve with recreational activities such as hunting, falconry, play-fighting and possibly archery, though this was more the domain of the lesser-privileged.

This education and service would continue until the onset of puberty, which for the average boy is about 12 years old, at which time he would be assigned to a knight or mercenary, becoming his squire and personal attendant in exchange for the opportunity to learn the knightly arts. It was at this point that his martial training started in earnest with a good grounding in the use of techniques both mounted and un-mounted, armoured and un-armoured, and also weaponry. This education continued until such time as the squire graduated (normally around 18 years), either into service as a Knight Bachelor or as a mercenary, the former being very much dependent on whether he could afford the 'commission' involved with becoming a knight, and all the necessary regalia that was associated with that position (armour, war-horse, etc.). The less socially privileged and/or less wealthy squire was left with the possibility of becoming a mercenary, remaining as a squire for an indefinite period, or choosing to further his knowledge by entering into the service of other knights/mercenaries, or even paying for the privilege of being taught under a Master of Fence.

The progression from page to squire and then to knight/mercenary was by no means inevitable, and it could be halted at any stage. Good evidence for this comes from the 14th Century poet Chaucer (son of a wealthy vintner and so undoubtedly merchant class) whose career began as a page to King Edward III's second son Lionel, Duke of Clarence. He later became Clarence's squire, but he was never knighted. It should be observed that, whilst it was theoretically possible for any free man of substance to be knighted, by the beginning of the Renaissance it was almost unheard-of for this to happen to a boy who was not from knightly lineage and supported by a wealthy and noble patron/family. The less fortunate, especially those not from noble backgrounds, could certainly advance to the rank of Captain in an army (equivalent to Knight Bannerette) and thus lead troops, but further advancement was improbable.

It is highly unlikely that a Master of Fence was from wealthy nobility, otherwise he would have taken the title of Knight before Master. The title of Master is used in the context of a teacher in this instance, the study of fence being very much dependent upon either a sympathetic patron or wealthy family, in order that support was provided whilst teaching the Art of Fence. Whether a Master of Fence could make a living teaching the Art independent of such support is conjectural but not impossible, if the Master's reputation was such that students actively sought him and were prepared to pay for the privilege of studentship.

Today it is easy to forget that life before formal education and mechanised transport was so much more physical and generally very much harder. Without the apathy of the modern classroom, the pollution of industry, the nutritional degradation of food quality and the god-like medical interventions that somewhat negate Darwinianism, the average constitution of an individual was healthier than today and every day had the purpose and meaning of survival and not the drudgery of profit. Youths in training for knighthood at this time had much greater stamina, were physically stronger, and were more truly educated in many respects than is the case in our soft and comfortable modern society.

Even today, as in the 14th Century, the process of learning a martial art can help guide and strengthen an individual's constitution, but as I mentioned earlier, not without dedication and sacrifice. Unlike in late medieval Europe, there are now many superficial distractions that can easily lure us away from a single path. The early years of our lives are taken up by education, in expectation of a material wealth that has no social responsibility, unlike the situation in medieval Europe. Our culture today is more a reflection of our innate selfishness, and in addition to the significantly reduced risk of premature mortality, lessens the requirement to make a single choice of one's future life, so this commitment is made later and later until a point where no commitment is made at all. The result is indecision and eventually chaos, which appears to be where our current society is leading us all.

Unlike in modern life, if a practitioner wants to succeed in a martial art, the path is very straightforward and simple but also very strict. All who wish to achieve success, regardless of what type, have to model their lives around their art to the point they wish to attain. Not to do so will produce mediocrity and limited success, as we see everywhere in modern society. For some the art is about reaching a certain goal, be it for competition or personal confidence, but for the true practitioner it is about a lifelong journey getting progressively more interesting as the road is travelled further. Like any pastime, there are challenges to conquer and problems to overcome but how far a student progresses is the individual's personal decision. There are no short cuts, and all this book can hope to do is to make the decision, and the journey that succeeds it, easier though not necessarily quicker. Success very much depends on the commitment of the individual and these publications can give a significant insight into understanding the science of the Art. As such, learning the Art is very much a personal journey and not one that can be taught.

The anatomy and characteristics of the late medieval longsword

The medieval longsword evolved to be a complex and comprehensive weapon in both its design and application. The diagrammatic representation found later in this chapter refers to a generic design of late medieval longsword, where the overall length is governed by the height of the user and is taken from the floor to the solar plexus. All the aspects of this generation of sword are represented proportionally. The handle, measured from the outside edge of the pommel to the blade side of the cross guard, is approximately a third of the blade length when taken from the point of balance, so just shy of being a quarter of the total sword length, with the cross guard no wider than the length of the handle. If you know where you want the point of balance for the sword, you can extrapolate the approximate length of the handle. It must be stressed that these proportional reference points are approximate and small differences between swords must be expected, if for no other reason than because they are manufactured by hand.

The blade should have sufficient thickness to be fairly rigid and have a constant taper from the cross guard to near the point, turning in at the point to support the tip. Most examples of practical longswords from the 15th Century are remarkably light. Obviously the overall dimensions will affect the weight of any sword but generally the late medieval German longsword very much follows the Oakshott reference Type XVII.

With a training weapon, you do not want any form of sharp edge or point to your blade. We at the School of Traditional Medieval Fencing prefer a slightly rebated weapon to approximately 0.5mm or as near to sharp without cutting, and a button point ground during its manufacture. The blade should be as close to the original weight as possible, though this varies with length; but generally it should be less than 3lbs for a sword that is, for instance, 48" long. The balance of a sword is different from its weight as the balance is carried by the wrist and the weight by the elbow/shoulder. A sword can be heavy yet feel light, because of the balance relative to the forehand position.

If a sword was to represent a live/sharp blade, it would be very sharp along the last third or quarter to the point, and blunt, but not necessarily rebated, along its remaining length to the cross guard. There are examples of blades being sharp along the entire blade length, but practically speaking these are rare and they were unlikely to survive with regular use; this is why they are found in collections and usually in reasonable condition, since they were rarely used or were kept for ceremonial purposes.

Extensive research by Herbert Schmidt suggests that the ideal profile for performance in cutting and durability is what he calls the 'apple seed' edge, where the sides of the blade taper evenly (be they convex, flat or concave) and at the point of contact curve in to form the cutting edge, much like the pointed end of an apple seed, hence the name. When placing this into context, it does make sense as the process of normal sharpening by hand with a stone will give this profile, and as long as the surface area is minimised (the sword blade profile is not too thick for it), this constantly curving surface will provide the best all-round performance.

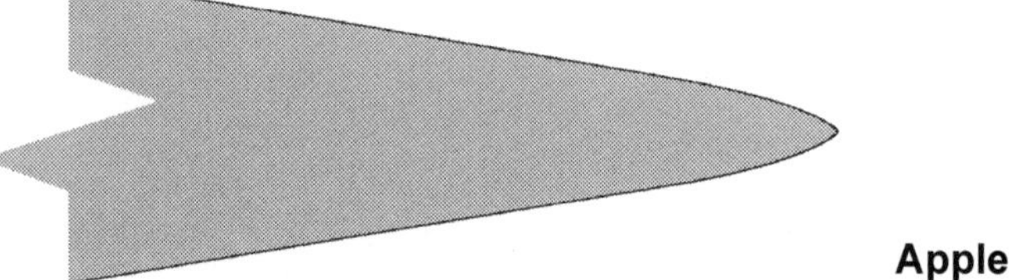

Apple Seed

By having a constantly diminishing surface area (as with the apple seed), the edge is supported by the curve; but surface resistance to cutting is reduced the deeper the cut is made until the apple seed edge is passed, and then the angle of resistance is at its lowest for the blade profile.

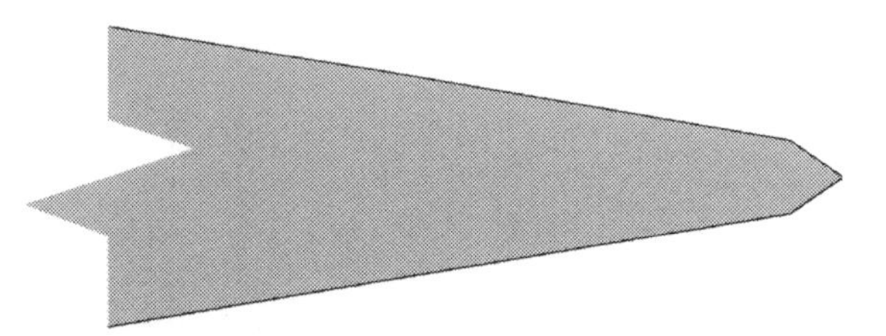

Wedge

By having a steep angle into the edge, although the edge itself is supported, the surface contact is forcing an opening much like a wedge, so offering resistance.

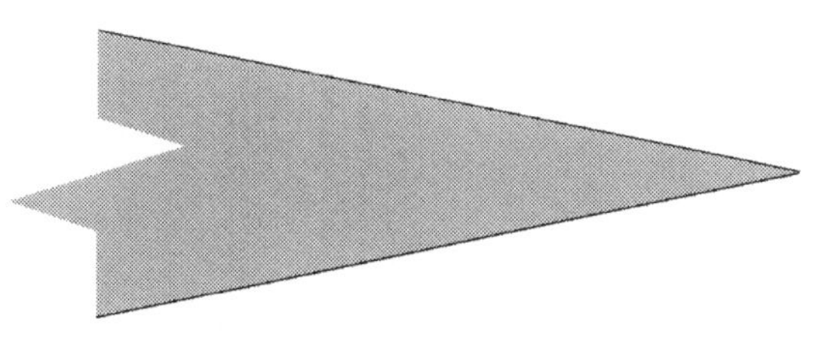

Narrow Taper

If the cutting edge were formed by following the angle of the blade to a point, although offering minimal resistance, this would not survive more than one or two cuts into clothing or thin leather, before becoming significantly blunt, because there is a reduced amount of material supporting the edge.

Sword anatomy

Sword anatomy refers to the names of the different parts of a sword. Below is a diagrammatical representation, followed by an explanation of what each name represents and its purpose.

Tang

The tang is the shouldered extension of the blade that resembles a tapered metal bar; it dictates the length of the grip and allows the pommel to be securely fastened to the sword. The tang and the blade are part of the same billet and would be drawn out into a taper during the forging process in such a way that the cross guard or quillion, being manufactured with a slot in the centre, would slide over the tang and be mounted securely by hammering it onto the tang at the shoulders and against the blade. The pommel, also manufactured with a rectangular hole along the centre, would then push onto the tang, being secured by **peining** over the end of the tang, so forcing the pommel tight onto the taper. In the diagrammatic representation below, the tang is highlighted by the broken line within the grip.

Pommel

The pommel is the metal weight at the handle end of the sword and used as a punching or hammering element of the weapon, but more importantly it acts as a counter-balance to the blade and its size and design very much depend upon the type and period of sword onto which it is attached. The weight of the pommel has a direct effect on all of the sword's characteristics and is a variable element in a sword's manufacture, being used to fine-tune many of a blade's dynamics. For example, some people prefer a heavy balanced blade, others a light balanced blade, and these adjustments are achieved by moving the point

Anatomy of the longsword

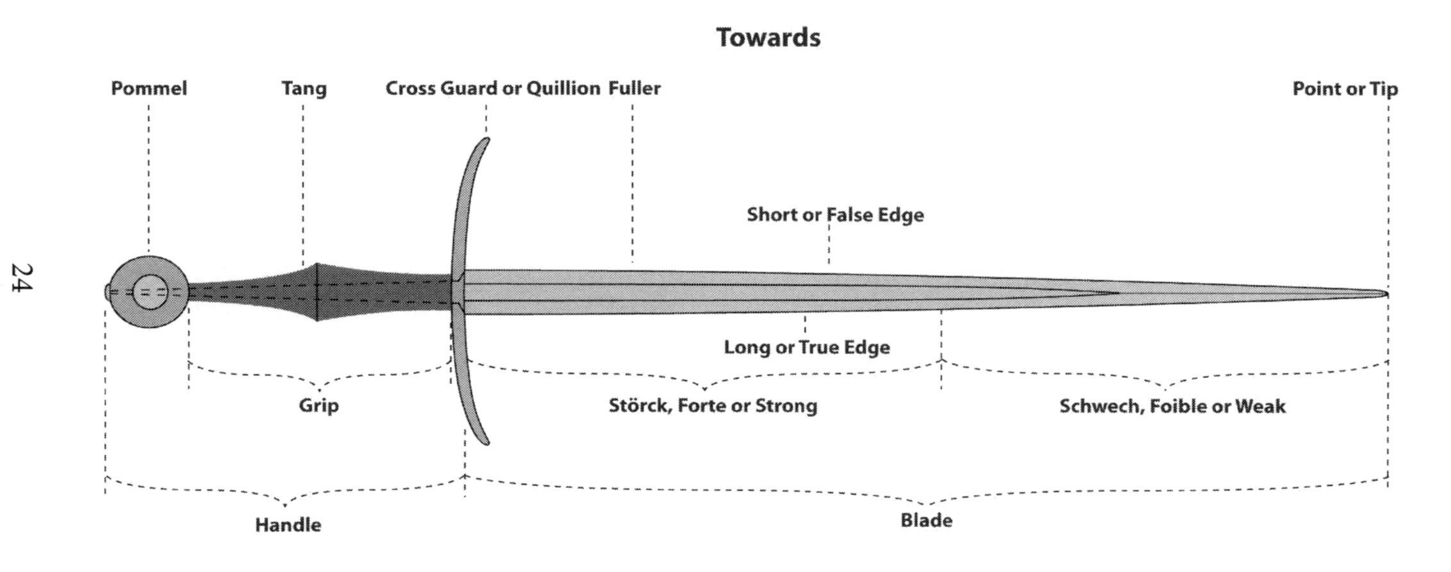

of balance relative to the forehand position on the grip. For a lighter balance, you increase the weight of the pommel so moving the point of balance closer to the hand; for a heavier balance you decrease the weight of the pommel thus moving the point of balance away from the hand.

Grip

The grip is the part of the sword where the hands spend most of their time, the length of the grip being dictated by the tang and affecting the size of the pommel: the longer the grip, the smaller the pommel for a set balance point. The grip is situated between the pommel and the cross guard or quillion and there are two general styles depending on the preference of the user, the type and the period of the sword. The shape can be either bottle or oval. The bottle profile has a raised section in the centre of the grip, tapering to the pommel and waisted to the cross guard or quillion, and looks very much like the grip on the diagrammatic representation opposite. The oval grip is similar to the shape of an elongated pine cone and although it tapers to either end from the fatter middle, it does not have the pronounced ridge of the bottle grip. Early grips were sometimes cylindrical, but these swords had much shorter handles. Grips are mainly formed in two halves from wood with a slot cut out for the tang and attached with a combination of glue, packing, leather, wire, etc. When the grip's finished shape was achieved it would be left as wood, covered in leather, bound with linen cord or wire, or a combination of all of these, and occasionally, if bound in leather, the grip could be embossed by tooling whilst wet.

Handle

The handle incorporates the pommel, the grip and the cross guard or quillion. The length of the handle is dependent upon the type and period of sword to which it is attached. Obviously its length is very much dictated by the length of grip and size/style of pommel.

Cross guard or Quillion

The cross guard or quillion, from this point referred to as the crossguard, protects the user from the opponent's blade during the **Winden** or in a **bind.** It acts as a convenient stop, and when used properly can cover the user's hands as well as allowing opportunities to manipulate the opponent's blade into a weak position. The crossguard can also be used as a hook or spike during striking when using two-handed, **halfswording**, or performing **hammer strikes**. As with the pommel, its weight and design depend very much upon the type and period of sword to which it is attached. Unlike the pommel, because the crossguard is so close to the forehand position, its weight is negligible relative to the balance of the sword; however, its length, if excessive, can obstruct and hinder the movement of the sword when in use, by fouling with the user's forearm and body. Generally, the crossguard is no longer than that of the overall length of the handle.

Blade

The blade makes up the greater part of the overall length of the sword and carries the edge that makes it what it is, a sharp weapon. The profile of the blade can vary depending on the type and period of manufacture and could be anything from oval, sharpened thin rectangular section, diamond section, or with multiple fullers, thus creating a multiple diamond section. Each has its benefits and weaknesses and all are relevant as viable sword blades. Regardless of section profile, the method of manufacture figures greatly in whether a sword will endure the rigours of use and there is evidence to suggest that a good blade would outlive its original lifespan by being updated with new furniture (pommel, grip, crossguard) in order to make it fashionable. Commonly, a refurnished blade would have been a family heirloom and passed down through many generations, conferring great spiritual value on a family name and increasing the credibility of an individual possessing it.

Early blades would be forged from a composite construction, having a soft folded iron core with forge-welded harder carbonised steel-like edges to allow flexibility for strength and durability for cutting/blocking. These blades were of reasonable quality, relatively cheap to manufacture and more commonly available, this style of sword originating from the Roman period.

From the 5th Century A.D. (and possibly earlier) to mid 11th Century, a method of manufacture was developed and used that consisted of multiple core pattern-welded blades, with twisted, folded and platted core elements of different iron types and forge-welded hardened steel-like edges. These types of blades provided very good all-round performance as any flaws in one material would be diluted by the other elements in the blade and multiple flaws were very unlikely to rest adjacent to one another. The best examples of this type of craftsmanship are found in old Saxon/Norse swords and beautiful patterns can be seen along the central core of the blade. It is believed that these are the blades, like Hrunting in the 8th Century poem 'Beowulf', that afforded the sword its ritualistic, spiritual and reverential demeanour in the developing medieval society, and they are most likely the source for blades such as Excalibur in the Arthurian legends. Today, swordsmiths such as Paul Binns are rediscovering these techniques and manufacturing beautiful pattern-welded blades, keeping these ancient traditions alive.

A method of carbonising iron, called cementation, was perfected around the 11th Century, and the result was a carbon steel manufactured with a suitably even density from which to draw sword blades. The cementation process consisted of several thin iron plates, between which was placed a carbon-rich powder derived from processed animal horn, ligament, rawhide, etc. This sandwich was surrounded by more of the same powder and placed in an air-tight container, possibly a metal box sealed with clay, being careful to omit any air pockets within. The temperature was raised to a yellow heat in a furnace for a set amount of time, possibly days, and the results of this produced a carbon rich iron-based material, similar to carbon steel. These sheets would then be cleaned, forge-welded together and from the resultant billet a folded steel blade drawn. The process of forging would harden the surface further, called work hardening, and resulted in a flexible and durable blade, without the complication of forge-welding dissimilar ferrous materials, as with the composite blades. If done properly, these blades could provide many years of service but because of the limited precision arising from the carbonising process, the quality of steel could vary between batches. There were only a few blade manufacturers who perfected this method and these were mainly Frankish swordsmiths, exporting crates of basic blades (blade and tang, no furniture) to countries all over Medieval Europe; on reaching their destination, they would be finished in the tradition and style of that area.

Fuller

The fuller is a channel forged along the centre of a blade, usually on both sides, and quite often mistaken as a means of making the blade more rigid or channelling blood. The fuller actually allows the sword to be lighter in weight and more flexible, without severely compromising its strength and rigidity. In the medieval period iron was difficult and expensive to manufacture and high grade iron even more so. Keeping the material use to a minimum was economically advantageous to the swordsmith and the fuller provides this opportunity, as well as improving the overall performance of the blade. The use of a fuller in modern training weapons has the additional benefit of keeping the weight to a realistic level whilst still maintaining a rebated and safe edge/tip.

Point or Tip

The point or tip of the sword blade, from here referred to as the tip, is the very furthest part of the blade where the profile diminishes to nothing. The later style of medieval swordplay, typically the German style, favoured the thrust and this most likely evolved because of increased use of more readily available mail and plate armour on the battlefield. As a consequence, the general blade profile went from being wide and flat, for cutting with heavy concussive strikes, to narrower and more diamond section at the tip for thrusting. The narrow point of contact, similar to that of a stiletto or roundel dagger of the same period, made the sword stronger at the tip and better for halfswording, acting as a lever between plate or forcing the rings open when thrusting through mail.

Long or True Edge

The long or true edge is the edge of the blade facing away from the user's arm when holding the sword on the grip, and is the edge more traditionally used for cutting, hence it being 'true'. It is called the long edge because of the long stroke adopted when cutting with it. Single edged weapons have only a long or true edge.

Short or False Edge

The short or false edge is the edge of the blade facing toward the user's arm when holding the sword on the grip and would only be found on a double-edged weapon. It is the edge not traditionally used for cutting, hence it being 'false'. One possible reason why it is called the short edge is because of the very short levering strike used when cutting with it.

Störck, Forte or Strong

The Störck, forte or strong, from this point referred to as the Störck, of the sword is the part from the middle of the blade length to the crossguard. It has this name because of the mechanical advantage gained relative to the position of the grip during a bind or block. The closer an opponent's blade can be drawn into the crossguard, the easier it is to control an opponent's threat, so a majority of blocks will take place within the Störck and will be led by the movement of the hands via the upper body.

Schwech, Foible or Weak

The Schwech, foible or weak, from this point referred to as the Schwech, of the sword is the part of the blade from the middle of its length to the tip. Although the Schwech is predominantly used for cutting, it is also the fastest moving part of the blade but, because it is furthest away from the hands, it is also the weakest and most easily controlled.

Sword characteristics

Sword characteristics refer to the physical properties of the sword. Below is a diagrammatical representation followed by an explanation of what each element represents and its dynamic effect on the overall character of a sword during use.

Point of Balance

The point of balance represents the centre of mass and so, as it is assumed that a longsword is symmetrical on one plane, the balance will be along this line of symmetry. The point of balance is gauged by pivoting the sword along the flat of the blade until a balance is achieved. The further down the blade the point of balance is from the crossguard the heavier the blade will seem on the wrist, as the offset mass in front of the forehand position (pivot point during use) will be creating a downward force. If you want a swinging blade, with a dynamic similar to that of an axe or hammer, then the point of balance should be closer to the tip. If a blade that moves quickly but has no cutting power or control is desired, then the point of balance should be close to the hand. For a generic late medieval German longsword, the balance wants to be between 2 to 3 finger widths (1 ½" to 2" or 37mm to 50mm) from the crossguard. This gives sufficient mass on the wrist to cut well without detriment to the tip speed, and still allows the user to feel where the blade is without it being uncomfortably heavy.

Percussive Node and Perceptive Node

The nodes of percussion and perception are the points along the sword that the nodes of a standing wave occur and represent the frequency of the sword itself. They appear along the edge plane of the blade and can be induced by holding the blade lightly in the forehand against the crossguard and tapping once the flat of the blade at the centre of the sword with the heel of the other hand. When looking along the edge of the blade, a point towards the tip should not appear to be vibrating. This is the percussive node and is where the static bind should occur, being between the last third to quarter of the blade.

To deduce the perceptive node is a little more difficult, but by pinching the flat of the blade at the percussive node, letting the sword hang from this point and tapping once against the flat of the blade as before, it should be possible to see the perceptive node within the confines of the grip. Ideally this node will be somewhere forward of the centre of the grip, or at least between the pommel and forehand position. The perceptive node needs to be near the forehand in order for positive feedback in the bind, at the percussive node, to be transmitted to the hands using the concept of **Fühlen**. In reverse, a displacement from the bind at the percussive node is made more positive because the initial movement originates from the perceptive node, so reducing the sword's flexibility as the action and reaction both occur about these nodes, thus making the transfer of energy more efficient.

Characteristics of the longsword

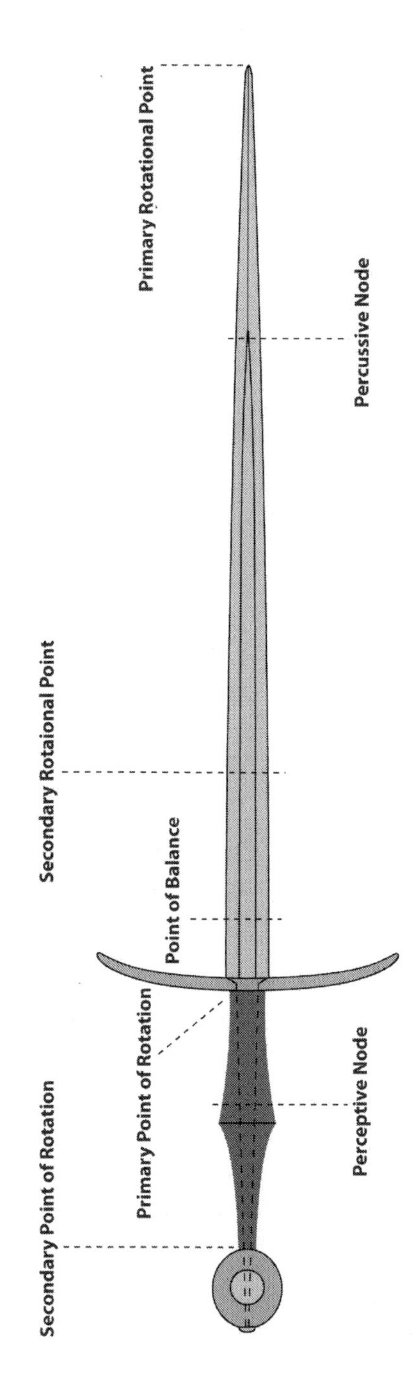

Primary Point of Rotation and Primary Rotational Point*

The rotational characteristic about the primary points offers an insight into the dynamic of a sword and whether it is suitable for use in the Winden. The primary point of rotation is the point where the forehand's thumb and forefinger restrain the sword about the grip close to the crossguard. It is called the primary point of rotation because, when winding or turning the sword whilst keeping the point along the centre, this is where the movement originates from.

The primary rotational point is the place along the line of the blade, not necessarily within the confines of the blade itself, where the primary point of rotation pivots. To find the primary rotational point, it is necessary to pinch the sword across the edge plane at the primary point of rotation and, allowing the sword to hang freely from this point, move the hand back and forth perpendicular to the edge plane in time with the natural dynamic of the sword, so creating a wave effect and revealing the pivot node. This action represents the frequency of the mass distribution of the sword about the forehand position and the node may occur anywhere along or even beyond the blade but, ideally, will be at the blade tip. In the German style, the use of Winden and rotational displacement is an important part of the system, so when displacing with the hands or winding it is vital that the tip stays centralised in order to maintain a threat. If a sword's primary rotational point is close to the crossguard or beyond the point of the blade, then the tip will also rotate, so removing itself from the centreline and giving its user a significant disadvantage.

Secondary Point of Rotation and Secondary Rotational Point**

Like the primary points, the rotational characteristic about the secondary points gives an insight into the dynamic of a sword when used for displacement of the tip around the **centreline**. The secondary point of rotation is the point where the pommel hand's thumb and forefinger restrain the sword about the end of the grip, close to the pommel. It is called the secondary point of rotation because, when displacing the point around the centre, this is where the movement originates from.

The secondary rotational point is the place along the line of the blade where the secondary point of rotation pivots. To find the secondary rotational point, it is necessary to pinch the sword perpendicular to the edge plane (across the flat of the blade) at the secondary point of rotation. Allow the sword to hang freely from this point and move the hand back and forth perpendicular to the edge plane in time with the natural dynamic of the sword, so creating a wave effect and revealing the pivot node. This action represents the frequency of the mass distribution of the sword about the pommel hand position, and the node will occur anywhere within the confines of the blade, ideally between the point of pivot and half-way down the blade length. You should notice that the oscillating frequency of the secondary points, in order to achieve a node, is higher than that of the primary points; or in other words you have to move the hand back and forth at a faster rate. The secondary points are vital to the German style of fence and allow us to establish how much ease of point displacement will be achieved when using the pommel hand to cut around an opponent's blade. If the secondary rotational point is too close to the tip, then insufficient displacement will occur naturally and so the user will have to overcome the dynamic of the sword in order to displace, making the movement slow and contrived. If the secondary rotational point is too close to the forehand, then there will be insufficient blade mass to moderate the displacement and so result in a sword that is difficult to control. A sword with good secondary rotation should have enough dynamic mass in front of the forehand to give sufficient feedback to the user, but not so little that the point is too mobile or so much that it inhibits the natural movement within the style used.

Conclusion

The sword is a complex tool and the information above is based on a generic design of sword from the late medieval period. All experienced sword fighters will prefer a combination of certain characteristics that complement their style of fence and tailor their sword to suit it. By following the generic proportions and achieving the point of balance suggested above, a blade should automatically have the correct dynamic regardless, within reason, of length. Specific characteristics can be fine-tuned with adjustments to the pommel and blade weight, but if the handle is too short or too long then one of the dynamics will suffer as a consequence. The initial proportions, which are set at the point of manufacture, are vital for a sword to have all the dynamic qualities desired for the Liechtenauer system. These recommendations are guidelines extrapolated from the combined research and experience of the author and by no means dictate the characteristics of every medieval longsword. As practitioners' experience and understanding improve with time and dedication to the Art, they will have the right to their own opinions so the recommendations above offer students a qualified starting point from which to hone their own skills and understanding.

* This characteristic was first brought to the attention of the author by Peter Johnsson and further developed and expanded by the author.

** This is a concept brought to the author's attention by Herbert Schmidt and further expanded by the author.

Training weapons and their respective strengths and weaknesses

As mentioned above, training weapons can have a diverse effect on how a technique might be interpreted, and finding the right balance between safety and authenticity can be complicated. Here is a general explanation of observations on training simulators and their respective strengths and weaknesses:

Wooden wasters

Positives:

- Cheap and easy to manufacture, though good examples can be expensive because of the type of wood used in order to give some durability to the blade, and the time and care taken to create sword-like characteristics. There are some nice laminated examples but they are bespoke and in consequence expensive.
- Can offer reasonable authenticity in the thrust and during winding and can be made to 'fit' the individual without much effort

Negatives:

- Often too heavy and it can be difficult to make the dynamic and balance accurate without reducing the effective durability
- Do not provide positive reaction in the strike or during a dynamic displacement (strike against a blade) as a result of having no percussive or perceptive nodes
- Because of the nature of the material, the feeling within the bind is dubious
- On striking with intent, these can be dangerous because of their rigidity and as a consequence of them often being blade-heavy and difficult to control.

Nylon wasters

Positives:

- Cheap, don't rust and don't suffer from wood-worm

Negatives:

- Have been known to break between the handle and the blade
- Too flexible in the bind and during striking, and though some now have a steel rod within the blade to reduce this, they are still far from realistic
- The fact they are made from nylon makes them too slippery in the wind and dangerously uncontrollable
- Too light and badly-balanced, with no discernible characteristics even remotely close to a steel sword.
- Have no realistic comparisons with a steel sword other than general dimensions and shape

Modified shinai

Positives:

- Made from four pieces of split bamboo bound together with a leather sock at each end, connected via a nylon cord. Readily available, cheap to buy and easy to modify; have been developed over a considerable time, being used as Eastern martial arts sword simulators
- If fitted with a wooden crossguard and counterbalanced properly within the grip, these can make good, cheap training weapons
- Not too heavy on the shoulder/elbow and, if balanced properly, give the appropriate dynamic for a beginner to understand the techniques without excessive effort
- Easy to control, can be used with intent and a significantly reduced risk of serious injury to a training partner
- Offer sufficient visual impression to be clearly visible and so allow the beginner to see what is happening, thus achieving good practice
- As tools to learn the basics and as general weapons to be used in a class situation, they offer a very good compromise

Negatives:

- Do not behave in an ideal way with regards to Winden; do not provide an accurate reaction during dynamic displacement since they have no percussive or perceptive nodes
- Being manufactured from split bamboo, they can suffer damage and

need to be regularly checked for signs of splintering

- Have no discerning long or short edge profile, so the nylon cord used to prevent them from flexing in the wrong direction must always be towards the user and represent the short edge of the blade
- Apart from the nylon cord, the only other reference the user has with regards to cutting along the edge is the crossguard, and in consequence it can sometimes be difficult for a student to cut in the proper way
- Students with smaller hands find the wooden crossguard inhibits the transition from true to false grip

Steel socketed shinai

Positives:

- Use a steel socketed handle and are balanced and weighted to resemble steel in all dynamic aspects with the exception of the percussive and perceptive nodes
- Split bamboo will absorb the shock experienced when striking, so significantly reducing possible injury
- Dynamic displacement is accurate though it cannot replace the rebated steel for realistic thrusting or winding from the bind
- The extra weight gives students an opportunity to increase their strength and control, and understand further the dynamic of movement when using a sword
- The steel crossguard makes it easier for users to discern whether they are cutting properly or not
- An improvement over the modified shinai when taking the false grip, as the crossguard will not inhibit the transition from true grip
- Shinai can be replaced independently of the handle in case of damage, making for a cheaper repair

Negatives:

- Expensive to manufacture
- Do not allow dynamic displacement in quite the same way as a steel sword because of the lack of a percussive node
- The nylon string must always represent the short edge
- Being made from split bamboo, the blade must be regularly checked for signs of splintering

Other shinai variations

Wooden crossguard with the sides of the split bamboo being taped together to form an 'edged' profile along the blade

Positives:

- Some reference to an edge.

Negatives:

- Although it is possible to comprehend the rationale behind this practice, in some respects the logic is fundamentally flawed as it defeats the object of having a safe training weapon that reduces injury when used with proper intent
- If modifying a shinai in this way, then why not simply use a wooden waster, as that is effectively what the shinai has become?

Heavy lead collar used on the blade side of the wooden crossguard

Positives:

- Still a shinai

Negatives:

- Shows no comprehension of how this has any benefit at all with regards to reproducing the characteristics of long swords
- Not only provides a very blade-heavy simulator, but also encourages incorrect intent, timing and body mechanics since users are constantly trying to overcome the incorrect dynamic of the weapon. It could be likened to fencing with a reasonably balanced hammer rather than a sword.

Feder

Positives:

- Safe in the thrust and have discernible cutting edges

Negatives:

- Too flexible, badly-balanced and badly-weighted
- Have no realistic dynamic characteristics with respect to a steel sword
- Too light and fast to force good technique and proper body movement

- The very aspect that makes the feder safe in the thrust is the same one that makes it useless in the bind/wind and unpredictable when striking

Rebated steel sword

Positives:

- If good examples, and made to the correct proportions, weight and balance, they cannot be bettered as training weapons, being what all other simulators aspire to copy

Negatives:

- Not suitable for beginners and purchase cost can be prohibitive
- Are easily damaged, if used improperly, and edges can become serrated to the point of breakage
- Cannot be used safely at speed and with intent when striking, or specifically in the thrust
- Only suitable for very experienced fencers in any situation outside form work and controlled drills

Summary

From personal experience I believe that, for the beginner, a modified shinai offers the best option as a starting simulator. For the intermediate fencer, the steel socketed shinai, with the correct weight and dynamic, is the most appropriate next stage as it is as close to a rebated steel sword in character without compromising safety, thus still allowing for use with proper time and intent. The next possible simulator option for an intermediate fencer is a well-made wooden waster. The ultimate simulator would have to be a rebated steel sword of correct proportions and characteristics.

Conclusion

Every practitioner aims to own a steel training weapon, and a good rebated steel training sword is unsurpassable with regards to historical accuracy in all aspects of fence. If a properly proportioned, accurately weighted and well-balanced training sword can be afforded, then I recommend using it for all form work and controlled drill movements from as early as possible in a student's development. However, if a suitably accurate steel training sword cannot be found, then using a bad example will be detrimental as the student will constantly be compensating for the weapon, regressing in development and struggling to understand the concepts and principles involved in the Art. Controlled or free sparring should not be performed with any steel training weapon, but rather with a shinai or waster, until a level of competence has been reached by which an individual can spar safely and in a controlled manner, taking into consideration the safety of not only of himself but also of his training partner. For a beginner, if regularly training, this level of competence could be achieved well within 5 years.

It is important always to use like against like, e.g. shinai against shinai, steel against steel. To train on differing simulator types is detrimental to weapon and technique alike.

Training the techniques contained within this manual

If a co-operative training partner can be found who remains true to the essence and reality of the situation when acting as an opponent, then the Liechtenauer techniques will occur quite naturally. It is important that, whilst training, proper intent is maintained and the temptation to pre-empt a training partner's actions when performing a technique is resisted at all times, otherwise the system will fail because each student is effectively seeing into the future and will no longer be striking or reacting in proper time or with proper intent. This is not helpful to anyone, especially the person trying to master that particular technique, and to assume, as a recipient, that an opponent will strike in a predictable manner is also foolish. These techniques are purely tools by which to understand the system; if students do not hold true to them they will never learn the Art.

Remember: Regardless of what type of long sword simulator is being used, shinai, wooden waster, rebated steel, etc., it represents a sharp sword and must be respected as such. If the threat represented by a sharp sword is ignored, and it is taken for granted by a student that there is no possibility of injury, then no individual can learn the Art as, in reality, serious injury will occur before there is an opportunity to gain understanding.

The subject of body protection is always controversial within the HEMA community and there will be varying opinions concerning this subject, but generally, when training, the best protection is common sense. The risk of injury can never be removed from HEMA, but the likelihood can be reduced to an acceptable level. Minor injuries must be considered inevitable with all physical activities, and for students to develop beyond the very basic application of the Art they must accept the possibility of injury and assume responsibility for that decision. What is important is that serious and life-threatening injuries do not occur, and every effort must be taken to prevent this by being a responsible practitioner and taking reasonable precautionary measures to prevent serious injury, not only to oneself but also to one's training partner. Prevention can be in the form of moderated force, reduced speed of movement, or physical protection, each being applied appropriately and with the consent of the parties involved.

Preventative practice should be applied to the lowest common denominator but not to the point of being detrimental to learning. If students are afraid and show no sign of improving then they are possibly not suited to HEMA. If you have students who are under 18 years of age then any possible risk MUST be reduced to a minimum regardless, unless parental (or equivalent) consent can be obtained, in which case you adapt appropriately.

To over-protect students is to provide them with a false sense of security and to deny them the acknowledgement and awareness of danger. To use insufficient protection will put students in the way of potential serious injury. When using non-ferrous simulators, in the majority of situations a pair of padded gloves and a fencing mask should accommodate every eventuality, but only when performing techniques outside the normal process of form work or controlled sparring. When performing techniques that present an obvious danger to students or their training partners, like any of the **Maisterhaw**, it is vital to show sense and use appropriate speed and force according to the protective equipment used and the experience of the practitioners. Never perform a committed thrust or strike to any part of the body unless the target is appropriately protected.

This system is not designed for self-defence, although it could adequately function as such; it is self-offence and as with all HEMA it is designed to kill or seriously maim, so show respect by using appropriately moderated force when applying the techniques. Control is essential not only for safety but also in understanding the Art. There is no place for aggression in the art of fence as aggression is the art of ignorance.

The Exposition of the Manual

As written by Johannes Liechtenauer, glossed by Sigmund Ringeck and further expanded, with additions, by Christopher Stride.

Here begins the knightly art of the longsword

Ringeck: "Here begins the exposition of the manual, in which is written the knightly art of the long sword, composed and created by Johannes Liechtenauer, a great master of the art. May God be merciful to him! He it was who had the manual written with cryptic and obscure words, so that the art should not become common knowledge. And these same cryptic and obscure words have been glossed and explained, as appears in this same little book, by Master Sigmund of the Ringeck family, who is currently fencing master to his most noble Highness Albrecht, Count Palatine of the Rhine and Duke of Bavaria, so that any man who already has experience of fencing from a different source may read and understand them."

Expansion:
So we can conclude that the initial lessons written in rhyming couplets from Liechtenauer were no more than crib notes for his student(s), and the gloss that Ringeck provides is not meant to be understood by the beginner; hence these expansions to assist students in their understanding of the art of fence. For Liechtenauer to have expanded on his notes beyond the rhyming couplets would have exposed the system that he had spent most of his life developing and perfecting, thus effectively undermining his own position not only with his patron, but also with any future possible employer. He would also have succeeded in devaluing his studentship, as the art behind his system would have become common knowledge. It is reasonable to assume that, by the time Döbringer (Nuremberg, Germanisches Museum, MS 3227a, dated c. 1389) expanded on the original verse, Liechtenauer had already died.

Introduction

The introduction to the manual:
(Liechtenauer) Young knight, learn to love God and to respect women, so shall your honour grow. Cultivate knighthood and study art, which will bring you renown, and conduct yourself honourably in war.
Wrestle well, take the lance, spear, sword and ***Messer*** *with manly courage. Strike hard! Rush in: meet your opponent or let him pass by, so that the wise may hate the one who is seen to be on the defensive.*
Rely upon this truth: all arts have a length and a measure.

Expansion:
Here we have the basis of the contemporary chivalric attitude, which is important to our understanding of the system. This is not the Victorian concept of chivalry, which has a somewhat romanticised interpretation derived from a fantasised Arthurian legend, but an actual reference to a 'higher art', introducing the concepts of honour and courage as being two of the necessary qualities of knighthood, not to mention a belief in a higher being, in this case 'God'. These qualities suggest that the art of fence is not just a physical or emotional journey, but also a spiritual one, by which a man might find a path to becoming a better person or knight.

Liechtenauer states: *"meet your opponent or let him pass by, so that the wise may hate the one who is seen to be on the defensive"*. This statement reflects the conviction underlying the belief to 'know and act' or the '**In des**', and not to dither in thinking about an action. He also makes reference to this being an art: *"Rely upon this truth: all arts have a length and a measure"*, which is interesting to consider, since when it is combined with the martial content within the manual below, this makes Liechtenauer's lessons, to my knowledge, the first reference in Europe to a system of fence being an art. This reference to length and measure goes beyond the system and encompasses all arts, giving us an insight into the sophistication contained within the culture, understanding and belief at that time. To my mind, not to grasp and try to comprehend the attitude of society at the time the original Liechtenauer treatise was taught is foolish. The very essence of the Art at that time reflects the culture and social hierarchy, and to discover the Art we have to understand the nature of the man who spoke the wise words we are trying to unpick, and to explore the mindset and general context in which these words were written. As with any language, the meaning of words changes with time, or one word can carry multiple meanings, so understanding the author can help us to decipher the true intention of his teaching.

General advice

This is a text containing many good and common lessons of the long sword. *If you wish to display art, go to the left and to the right with blows. And to go left [leading with] the right means that you have a great desire to fence.*

Ringeck Gloss:
Note well: this is the first lesson of the long sword, which is that you should learn to strike blows from both sides correctly, if you intend to fight well and with strength. Mark this, that if you intend to strike from the right side, you must ensure that your left foot is forward. If you are striking the **Oberhaw** from the right side, then follow the blow with your right foot. If you do not do this, your blow will be false and not accurate, because your right side will not come forwards. For this reason, your blow will be too short, and will not follow its correct path beneath itself to the other side before [your] left foot. In the same way, if you are striking a blow from the left side and do not follow the blow through with your left foot, your blow will also be false. So make sure that, whichever side you strike from, you follow the blow through with the corresponding foot. In this way, you will be able to strike all your blows correctly and with strength. And this is also how all other blows should be struck.

Expansion:
Remember the **True Times of Distance**, be they of method or distance, which are explained fully below. Here we have a reference to the method of striking in the time of the hand. Always strike with the hand before the body, before the foot/feet. To do otherwise is to put yourself at a disadvantage by always being in the **Nach** and not the **Vor**.

[This is] the text of a second lesson
He who strikes late will gain little benefit from the art. Strike late however you wish, no change will come to your shield. Do not hesitate to strike your opponent to the head or to the body. Fight with your whole body to achieve that which you greatly desire.

Gloss:
When you approach your adversary to fence with him, you should not look for his blow, nor should you wait to see how he will attack you. For all fencers who look and wait for their adversary's blows and intend to do nothing other than **Ersetzen** will gain little benefit from such art, for they will often be struck.
Item: Note well that in all your fencing you should use the whole strength of your body! And as you come in, strike him using your strength to the head and the body, so that he will not be able to use the **Durch wechseln** before your point. And as you strike, while binding with the sword, you should not forget to strike at the next opening that will be described to you in the description of the five strikes and in other places.

Expansion:
This does not say that you should blindly rush in regardless of where or what your opponent is doing, but more that when YOU are ready to fence, you must enter into distance with conviction and intent, with knowledge that you are true to your cause and confident in your ability. To wait for the action of your opponent is to place yourself in the Nach and so be chased, which is why someone who looks to do nothing but defend will often be struck. Also, have a care to be at the correct distance and enter with proper intent. A static guard should always be beyond the second True Time of your opponent, Time of Hand, Body and Foot, entering into the second True Time with the front foot into **Zornort** and finishing your strike in Time of Hand, the first True Time, completing the movement with the finish of the pass through with the back foot. Do not forget, from a static guard always enter along the centreline with the intention of performing a **Zornhaw**, to pre-empt or do otherwise is a false art. To abide by this rule will put you in the Vor.

Here we also have reference to the proper technique for striking, leading with the hands and providing force from the driving foot (what was the forward but becomes the back foot with the pass), through the hips, shoulders and along the arms to the tip. Movement, accuracy and speed before the strike come from the hands, wrists and arms, but they are also your weakest elements, so take care to remove their weakness as you make contact by bracing the arms in a strong position; not locked straight but also not bent, and therefore strong. Control in the strike comes from the shoulders, waist and hips. Strength and distance are controlled from the knees and feet. I praise the student who leans upon the point.

As entry into distance is made, and so the start of the strike commences, we have a reference to being strong along the centre, maintaining a threat to the head and body so as to make disengagement by your opponent impossible, because to do so would result in his defeat. When opportunities arise from the bind or during the fence, take them. Do not fall into the Nach but maintain the Vor and take advantage of your opponent's weakness, applying the Maisterhaw as you do so.

Addition:

Important Principle:

The True Times of Distance

True Time of the Hand, Body, Foot and Feet,
Follow this order and my praise you will meet.
The fewer the order, the closer you stand,
At the end of a strike you must finish in Hand.

The four True Times of Distance represent the distance between you and your opponent relative to the amount of time it would take to cover that distance. Each example starts from a position with the right foot forward, if you are right-handed, or the left foot forward if you are left-handed. They are as follows:

The first True Time:

> **Time of Hand** is the distance at which you can hit your opponent without leaning forward with your body or stepping with the feet, resulting in a movement consisting of no more than a straightening of the arms, with regards to a sword used with two hands, or forward arm in the case of a single-handed weapon.

The amount of time it takes to strike in Time of Hand is very small and the broadcasting of any offensive movement towards your opponent, and towards you, is kept to a minimum. This is the most dangerous position to be in, and should typically represent the finishing distance of every successful strike when your balance is centred (i.e. not leaning forward).

The second True Time:

Time of Hand and Body is the distance at which you cannot reach your opponent by just extending the arms (Time of Hand) though it does not require you to move either foot in order to effect a strike. A strike is achieved by bending the front knee and leaning forward. This includes **Extending Forwards** and represents the Zornort, or the distance at which you should be striking from or have engaged into the bind. To bind at any closer distance is foolhardy and should be avoided unless already performing a Winden or entering with the intent to halfsword, grapple or wrestle at the sword.

The third True Time:

Time of Hand, Body and Foot is the distance by which you cannot reach with the hand or leaning forward with the body and so need to move either foot forward (singular step) in order to effect a strike. This is proper facing distance, the distance by which you stand in a static guard against your opponent and from which you enter into the fight distance proper of Time of Hand and Body with the Zornort by using a **half-step**.

The fourth True Time:

Time of Hand, Body and Feet is the distance at which you are no longer in Time of Hand, Body and Foot. This can be any distance between the third True Time and another country! It is literally too far away to do anything with reasonable intent using the weapon you have, but is a useful reference when used in consideration to an opponent with a different weapon. For example, if you are using a single sword and your opponent a pole weapon, when he is in the second True Time you are likely to be in fourth, giving him a greater advantage of distance relative to intent, and thus he can present a threat much more effectively than you.

The True Times of Distance go hand in hand with the True Times of Intent, which we will cover in the Grade 3.

Addition:

Important Principle:

The Centreline Concept

The centreline is the key to your fight,
Understand this and you'll never take flight.
It runs straight from them through the centre of you,
Where your line of intent and your feet follow true.
With a threat from above you relinquish the line,
Form another with a side-step in a single time.
But a threat from below you must challenge your foe,
And displace them away from what they know.

The concept of the centreline is universal with regards to all martial arts but only a few understand beyond natural ability. The principles within this concept allow you to decide whether to challenge or move the centre according to the position and line of intent of your opponent.

The generic centreline is an imaginary vertical line that runs along the horizontal plane from the centre of your mass through to the centre of your opponent's. It represents the shortest distance between you both and it is along this centreline that any intention must travel. Any entry along the centre with the intention of keeping the centreline we call 'challenging the centreline' (see Zornhaw and **Schilhaw**). It is only if this line is lost due to being in the Nach, as a consequence of a threat from the high line, that 'moving the centreline' provides a solution (see **Krumphaw** and **Zwerhaw**).

The position of an individual's specific centreline is dictated by the feet, and more precisely by the heels. If you draw a straight line through the heels then this line should follow the horizontal element of the generic centreline, with the front foot being in line with the centreline, towards your opponent, and the rear foot 90° to the centreline, facing outward. If this is not the case, then you will be off-balance with your intent, and any strike or extending forward you attempt will become your disadvantage. There will be moments during transition where your feet are moving and these should be for two purposes only, to enter along the centre or to traverse in order to find a new one. The completion of a movement should conclude with both your heels being along the centreline, as mentioned above, and through the centre of your opponent, as with the generic centreline.

End of Addition

A second lesson.
Hear what is bad: do not fight on the upper line on the left, if you are from the right; and if you are from the left, you will limp when you fight on the right.

Gloss.
Note well, this lesson concerns two persons, a left-hander and a right-hander. Pay good attention: if you, a right-hander, come to fence with your adversary and wish to strike him, do not strike your first blow from the left side, for this is weak and will not be able to withstand a strong binding action. For this reason strike from the right side, in this way you will be able to use your sword strongly with art to achieve what you wish. In the same way, if you are a left-hander, do not strike from the right side, because it is incorrect use of the art for a left-handed man to strike from the right, just as it is for a right-handed man to strike from the left.

Expansion:
Play to your strengths and do not place yourself at a disadvantage. If you are right-handed, then your first attack must come from the right side and because your right hand is punching through, driven by the right shoulder pushing forward, followed by the hip and then the foot, your sword will find more strength and better length in the strike. Practise the Maisterhaw from both sides, but when from a static position, enter into fence from your right if you are right-handed, and your left if you are left-handed. Liechtenauer mentions something here that Ringeck has not clarified: *"Hear what is bad: do not fight on the upper line on the left, if you are from the right"*. I think what Liechtenauer is getting at here is not to cross your body in the high line, e.g. if your left foot

is forward do not bind or fight on the upper left line, and vice versa. This is possible, though not ideal, with the lower line, from the **Pflug** into the Schilhaw for instance, as you can control your opponent's threat with your body mass, but it is not advisable in the upper line, from the **Ochs** into a Zwerhaw, as the turning moment experienced about the feet is above the body's centre of mass and will cause you to be off-balance and in an unrecoverable position.

Addition:

Important to technique:

Holding and Moving the Sword

Gentle hands persuade your weapon true,
Firm intent at point when striking through.
Grace of movement is the art within the fight,
Forced position will give you nought but flight.

When gripping the sword out of contact, do so with a gentle hand. Do not dictate its movement but persuade it with a flowing dynamic of your whole body; this will make you not only efficient in defence but quick in offence. Use the characteristics of the weapon to your advantage and it will respect you. Overcome its natural movement with force and you will be punished. I praise the student who has found art in movement.

The foregrip and pommel grip during movement should be with the thumb and fore/middle fingers in the right and left hands. This allows a large degree of movement within the palm of the hand whilst maintaining a secure hold upon the handle. The forehand should hold the foregrip close to the crossguard, but not necessarily against it, and the pommel hand should hold the pommel grip on the very end of the grip, cupping the pommel in the palm. Your sword handle should provide you with an appropriate profile for this to occur naturally. Not to take advantage of the full length of handle is foolish, and even though some profess that having the hands close together is the right position, it is weak and compromises the manoeuvrability and control of the point. The forehand and pommel hand should sit either side of the perceptive node within the handle which, in a good blade, is usually at, or slightly forward of, the centre of the grip. This allows you a much greater sense of Fühlen within the bind.

At the point of contact the entire hand must grip tightly, in order that the whole body weight be pushed through the tip, controlling the sword with the shoulders and hips and letting your feet naturally move beneath you to the centreline, so maintaining balance. By striking in this way, you will increase the effective mass of the blade to that of your body and your opponent will find it difficult to resist your will.

In addition to this, the hands should always be in front of the chest and never forward of the shoulder relative to the body line. When thrusting or extending the blade forward, always do so by turning the shoulders and not reaching with the arms. If your hands do extend forward of the shoulder you will be weak, easily controlled, and find it difficult to resist the will of your opponent.

Addition:
Important to technique:
The True and False Grip
The true grip is the long edge cutting way,
The false grip is the short edge cut I say.

There are two types of grip used in the system, the true and the false grip. Both are designed to provide the best grip for the type of application used. The true grip is mainly for long edge strikes, the false grip for short edge strikes.

The **true grip** is the same as if you were holding a hammer or an axe. The thumb and fingers are in line with the flats of the blade, the crossguard being aligned with the furthest forward surface of the forearm.

The True Grip

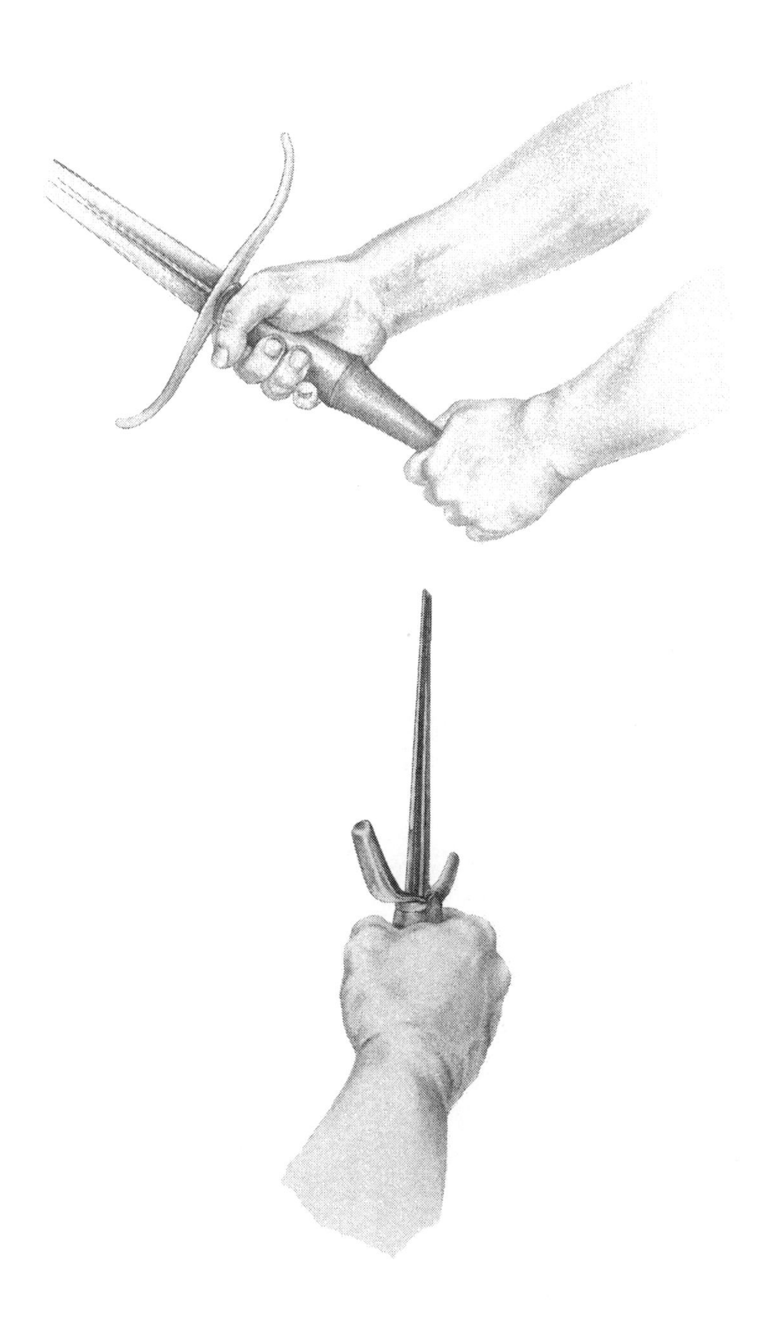

The **false grip** is effectively a 90° clockwise rotation (when viewed from the pommel) from the true position; it is achieved by turning the sword within the forehand with the pommel hand. The crossguard should now be perpendicular to the line of the forward-most surface of the forearm and the thumb should be along the flat of the blade. This provides support to the strike or thrust, and allows you to maintain the correct wrist orientation in both hands when sweeping the sword grip from your right to your left side (which is when the transition between true to false grip usually occurs), whilst maintaining a forward threat with the point. At no time should the hand be out of alignment with the forearm, and bending the wrist in any direction other than back or forth along the thumb-line of the forearm is weak and should be avoided at all costs. This transition from true to false grip occurs before a strike or during entry (e.g. during the Winden), never at the point of contact with the cut or thrust in the strike itself; the change of grip should have occurred by that time.

The False Grip

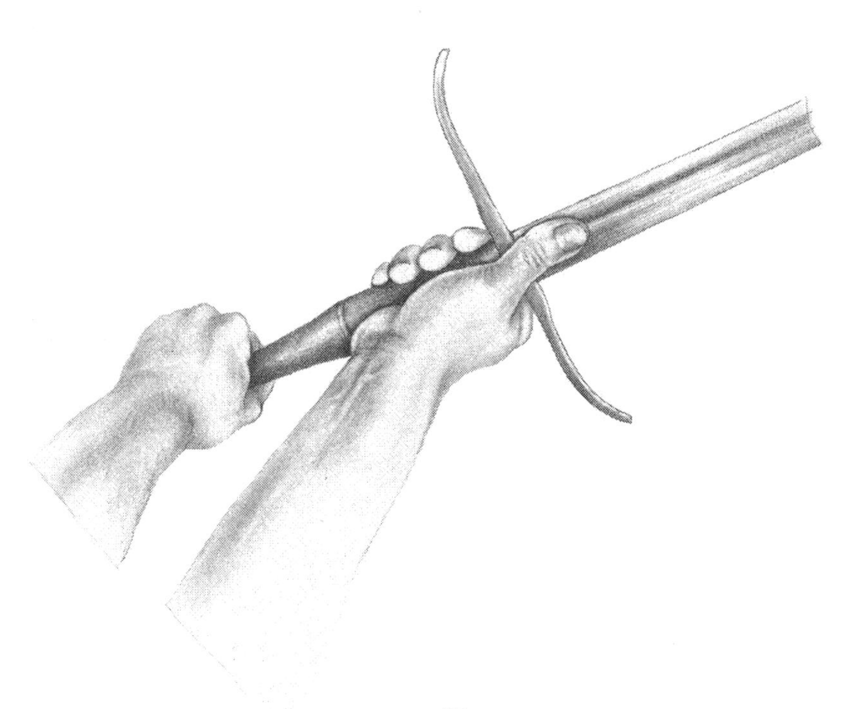

Addition:
Important to technique:
Cutting and Guarding/Blocking
The edge is for cutting, off edge your defence
Defend with the edge? You show ignorance!

The sword is your defence and your attack; the edge is vulnerable to damage because of the nature of the sword design and the desire to keep its weight to a minimum, whilst maintaining usability. You must cut true with the edge, in line with the blade, and push through onto the point. Defence should occur 'off edge', meaning not in line with the edges of the blade, and should never be a static occurrence but always a dynamic transition from one attack to another. Although there will be situations when the edge will become damaged, probably because of an opponent ignorant of the Art and blocking with a cut, this must be kept to a minimum, as every nick is a weak point and could considerably diminish the longevity of your blade, as well as rendering it useless as a training weapon. If you are fencing properly, the natural movement between positions should mean that you are constantly deflecting off edge when engaging with your opponent's blade. This does not mean that you are blocking with the flat, but shedding a threat away from you whilst moving your sword to present one anew on a different line. Any physical block would occur as a consequence of entering deep into your opponent's time and catching him early in his movement in order to wind or wrestle, with this type of block occurring within the Störck, and it would conclude against the crossguard; but even here you would be turning the edge away as you displace during entry.

End of Addition

Principles: 'Vor' and 'Nach'

This is the text, and a lesson about the principles 'Vor' and 'Nach'
The two concepts 'Vor' and 'Nach' are the wellspring of all art. Mark also the terms 'schwech' and 'störck' as well as the word 'In des'. In this way you will learn to fight and to defend yourself using art. But if you are easily frightened, you will never be able to learn to fence.

Gloss:
Take heed, before all else you should understand the 'Vor' and the 'Nach', for these two things are the source from which all the art of fencing proceeds. Therefore understand that 'Vor' means that you must move before your opponent with a strike or a thrust to his opening, before he can attack yours. He will then be forced to set aside your blade. In the same way, when you come to the setting aside of the blade, move your sword quickly from one opening to another, so that your actions will prevent him from being able to achieve his intent. But if he runs in at you, forestall him by using wrestling before he can.

Expansion:
The Vor and Nach are vital principles in the Liechtenauer system. These tie in with an earlier reference to the Vor and Nach in the general advice section above, and they are a good example of why and when you are challenging or moving the centreline.

The **Vor** literally means 'before', or as I prefer to consider it, 'lead'. The description above is accurate; move first, present the initial threat to any opening within the centreline before your opponent. Your opponent will be forced to defend himself by displacing the threat away from the centre with a **Versetzen** and so take the Nach. If your opponent initiates entry, then do not allow yourself to be put into the Nach and be chased, but retake the centre by presenting a counter-threat, so retaking the Vor at the first possible opportunity by using one of the Maisterhaw and/or Winden from the bind. If your opponent runs inside the point before you can deny him the opportunity, then take heed and look to enter into wrestling, achieving the Vor again by denying control of the centre to your opponent.

Gloss:
And now note the meaning of 'Nach'.
Take heed: if you are not able to achieve the 'Vor', wait for the 'Nach'. These are the counters to any attacks which he may make against you. And note this; if he moves first so that you have to set aside his blade, so make use of your Versetzen as he comes in, quickly, to reach the nearest opening. In this way you will strike him just as he makes his move. This will gain you the Vor and he will

be left with the Nach. In addition, while using Vor and Nach you should pay attention to how you should use the concept of simultaneous action against the Schwech or the Störck of his sword. And note: from the hilt of the sword up to the middle of the blade is the Störck of the sword, and with this you may resist if your opponent binds your sword there. Further, from the middle of the blade to the point is the Schwech of the sword, and with this you will not be able to withstand [a bind]. If you understand this concept correctly, you will be able to fight and defend yourself using the art; and indeed this is how princes and lords learn, so that they may triumph using this same art both in play and in earnest. But if you are easily frightened, you will never learn the art of fencing. If your heart is stupid and cowardly, it will achieve nothing, since it will be defeated by any art.

Expansion:
'The Nach literally means 'after', or as I prefer to consider it, 'chase'. Again, the description above is accurate. The Nach represents a counter to an initiative your opponent presents, as opposed to a block or purely defensive reaction. In this way you should never find yourself defending, but constantly looking to present a counter attack in order to achieve, or regain, the Vor.'

Here, Ringeck introduces two other vital principles of the Art, the Fühlen and In des. These allow you to take advantage of the characteristics of your opponent's swordplay and use them to regain the Vor. (We will expand further on these principles in Grade 3.) We also have the introduction of the concept Störck (weak) and Schwech (strong) in relation to the sword blade. The reference to weak and strong is also used to describe the force presented by your opponent so we shall refer to the positions along the sword blade as Störck and Schwech. We shall use weak and strong when referring to force used. It is important to understand these differences, as it is from them that the Fühlen and In des evolve. It is not necessary to expand on these elements at this time as they are more appropriate for a later grading.

Again Ringeck brings the concept of Art back into the system: "...you will be able to fight and defend yourself using the art; and indeed this is how princes and lords learn, so that they may triumph using this same art both in play and in earnest." By making reference to princes and lords, we could extrapolate that it is the Art that helps denote this social class from any other. To say "...

triumph using this same art in play or earnest" is interesting and I believe helps differentiate between the Liechtenauer and other systems of the same period. This is an art because it is not just practical in the real world but also recreational, challenging your own understanding and ability and not just that of your opponent. The desire to fence for the sake of fencing and not purely for need does suggest to me that the Art not only has influence within the social class of that period but also possesses a spiritual role in personal development and self-understanding. The enthusiasm for and courage within the Art evolves with training and experience into wisdom and maturity, something that is clearly observed whilst practising fencing for many years.

The Maisterhaw

The five secret blows

[This is] the text giving the five blows
This is the lesson of the five blows from the right hand. Who could it be that we promise cheerfully to repay through our art?

Gloss:
Note well: the manual describes five secret blows, which are unknown to many masters of the sword. You should only learn to strike these from the right side against him who opposes you. See if you can strike the man with your first attack using one of these five blows. An opponent who can break these blows without suffering injury will be praised by the master of this manual, and his art will be better rewarded than that of another fencer who is unable to counter these five blows. In the descriptions of the five blows below you will find how to perform each one.

Expansion:
The five secret blows are the Maisterhaw, or master strikes.

Ringeck re-enforces his previous statement of using these from the correct side for your hand (right side for right-handed fencer, left side for left-handed fencer) against someone who opposes you, or in other words, a static guard or position. They are a strong and safe method of entry and allow you to get into the second True Time with the possibility of victory in the **first intention**, or Vor into the second intention (the counter from the entry, the entry being the first intention).

The importance of the Maisterhaw cannot be stressed too strongly. They are the back-bone of the system and must be practised and understood in the minutest detail with regards to the physical movement, the principles that dictate that movement and the practical application of that movement.

All other techniques stem from the Maisterhaw and to understand this is to understand the system, which is why when Ringeck rewards those who can counter the five Maisterhaw, he does this because they have a significant understanding of the Art.

Here we will only be dealing with Maisterhaw against a static guard, and not the dynamic pieces associated with them. These additional pieces are not appropriate for a new student and will be covered in later gradings.

Addition:
Important to application:
The Zornort
Use this entry and be sure of true intent,
Along the centreline, ensuring wrath is meant.

Here we must introduce the concept of Zornort, or 'point of wrath', a transitional position which we use to gain entry from a static guard. The easiest way to achieve this is to start from the Pflug (as explained in the section on 'The Four Guards' below). From the Pflug, we gauge our entry into the second True Time with a half-step (step with the front foot) forward along the centreline. In doing so, you must ensure that the half-step you have taken brings you comfortably into the second True Time. Both shoulders must be forward, perpendicular to the centreline, and the arms strong (NOT locked straight), hands low and point maintained along your opponent's eye line. The body weight is forward, both front and rear leg flexed, with the forward leg controlling the weight and the rear leg pushing forward. This position is called the Zornort; it presents a strong entry along the centreline and forces your opponent to consider the threat presented, but do not forget that it is a transitional position and thus the forward dynamic of the entry must not be lost with hesitation. Keep coming forward along the centreline, with the intention of performing the Zornhaw, though ready to strike any of the other Maisterhaw at any time during the process (with the exception of the **Schaytler**), and do not waver from this intention unless you are threatened before you can safely conclude the Zornhaw. It is this **Single Time** dynamic point of transfer, from entry (Zornort) to strike, that will initiate all of the Maisterhaw in the following examples.

Addition:

Important to technique:

Extending Forward and Drawing Back

Extend not the shoulder beyond the knee,
Or it will be the floor that you will see.
To recover from forward, if extended you be,
As you straighten the front, so bend the back knee.
For drawing, remember the back foot's your guide,
To go beyond this, you must change your side.
But do not forget that this law still applies
The knee is your stop, the floor your demise.

Extending Forward:

This is a general rule. When reaching or extending forward, be careful not to allow the shoulder to extend beyond the forward knee or you will overbalance. To bend at the waist when extending is weak, and will also cause you to overbalance. When extending forward, thus pushing with the blade or at the tip, do so by flexing the front knee with strong arms and push with the shoulders from the back leg. This is achieved by maintaining a straight line from the shoulder, through the hip to the heel of the back foot, so if the left heel is back it should form a straight line between the left hip and shoulder, and vice versa. There should be a firm anchor point from the heel of the back foot, which is why the back foot must be perpendicular to the centreline, and unless you are preparing to pass through with a step, the back foot provides the point whence the force is applied from the ground, through the strong muscles of the legs, torso, through the shoulders and onto the tip.

N.B. The front foot should always be pointing towards your opponent along the centreline, as mentioned earlier, and the reason for this concerns balance. Because the mass of the body, and thus the force and control of any movement through to the tip of the sword, is controlled by the bending of the front leg, the direction in which the front leg bends is dictated by the foot. If your front foot is pointing away from the intended target then the bending of the leg will throw your body away from the centre and consequently off-balance; this action also stresses the knee joint, as you try to compensate by twisting the body to maintain the centre. If the foot is in line with the centreline, then the knee is bending in its designed direction enabling the body to follow this line, and the appropriate force is applied with complete control, using the heel of the back foot as an anchor (as mentioned previously).

Drawing back:
From extending forward, it is important that drawing back can be achieved with speed and agility, passing through a point of neutral balance (i.e. weight evenly distributed between both feet and upper body in an upright position), thus giving the opportunity for a change of direction should it be necessary. If you are extended forward, the rear leg/hip/shoulder is straight, with forward weight and distance controlled by bending the front knee. If we reverse this so that you are drawing back, with the weight backward, the front leg/hip/shoulder is straight and the extent of your draw controlled by the back knee, so changing the dynamic from forwards to backwards. To recover from either the extended or drawing position into a neutral balance, you need to use a combination of straightening the bent leg and bending the straight leg. When passing through the neutral position both knees should be slightly bent, as in the guard stance, and ready to pass back, forwards or traverse in either direction at any time necessary. In order for you to maintain balance, the rear shoulder should not extend beyond the back foot, and it is unlikely that you will ever need to draw back further than this point before passing back; however, should this need arise, there is the possibility of turning the feet during transition from the forward foot pointing towards your opponent (and the rear foot perpendicular), to the rear foot pointing away from him (and your forward foot perpendicular, effectively identical to the extending forward but with the threat behind). You are thus preparing to shed a blow away should your situation require it, ready to re-engage by leaping into **Ringen** or similar.

So for both the forward and backward stance, a general rule can be applied: For recovery from both extremes, bend the straight leg and straighten the bent leg simultaneously. When in either position, do not extend the shoulder beyond the furthest extended lower body part. (For the forward extension this is the knee, for drawing backward this is the foot, forward being dictated by the direction of the foot and the front foot being the one along the centreline.) Always enter into the neutral position with both legs bent, as is correct for that position, regardless of which direction the transition is in.

Additional:

Important to technique

The True Cross

The True Cross is the position that you feel within the bind,
The desire not to drop or not to lift and cut behind.
The pressure that you feel must be square against their blade,
Look for this position when from the bind a thrust is made.

The True Cross is a neutral position within the bind where neither party feels any particular inclination to rotate over or under the point of contact, and as you apply pressure against your opponent within the bind you will feel an equal and opposite reaction to your action in order to maintain an equilibrium. If your opponent binds against the Störck of your sword with his Schwech, as you apply an equal and opposite pressure you will notice your blade will have a tendency towards rotating over your opponent's, because the force you apply is stronger relative to the force he can control. If, in contrast, you bind against his Störck with your Schwech you will feel a tendency for your hands to pass beneath his blade because you cannot control the force they apply. The point at which the blades cross within bind, where neither you nor your opponent feels anything more than an equal and opposite force when applying pressure, is called the True Cross and usually occurs when displacing a thrust into your lower line with the Schilhaw.

End of Addition

Position of the Zornhaw

1. Zornhaw

This is the Zornhaw, and the techniques [to be used with it].
If your adversary strikes you from above, your point will threaten him using the Zornhaw.

Gloss:
Note that, if your opponent strikes you from above from his right side, you should strike a strong Zornhaw in return with the long edge, also from your right shoulder. If his sword is weak, then make a long thrust with your point to his face. Be sure that you will strike him.

Expansion:
The Zornhaw, or the 'strike of wrath', is the most important strike of all the Maisterhaw and should constitute the beginning of any entry from the second True Time into the first, travelling through the Zornort whilst claiming or threatening the centreline, depending on the opposing guard or position. It must be stated here that the Zornhaw, though the simplest of the Maisterhaw with regards to movement, is the most difficult strike to execute properly, its effectiveness being dependent on the timing of the various stages of movement. It is also the least likely of all the Maisterhaw to be executed to the point of conclusion, because your opponent is very unlikely to allow you the opportunity to complete it without opposition. That said, it is the only strike that will provide you with the opportunity to enter safely from a static position, and if not successful in the first intention it will give a definite advantage in transferring to the other Maisterhaw. The Zornhaw is a 'challenging the centreline' strike. In this example, you are both starting from a static guard, you with your right-hand in the foregrip and left foot forward, standing in the Pflug. If you are a left-handed fencer, then you must have your left hand in the foregrip and the right foot forward.

The Zornhaw is executed as follows: After passing through the Zornort your weight must continue forward, over the front foot, drawing the hands back in towards the body whilst doing so and bringing the right shoulder back slightly. Effectively you draw the body onto the hands relative to their original position. As the back foot lifts for the pass along the centreline, the hands should be punched forward with the right shoulder squaring up, achieving the position of Zornort again, at the point of contact, and recovering the strike with the right foot stepping down again on the centreline, now as the front foot. It is not specifically a strike or thrust but a combination of the two, with no great radial or axial movement of the blade but more a punch forward along the centreline parallel with the floor, the power being generated from the tensing of the upper body at point of contact as you enter into the Zornort on the other side. The length of the strike (distance travelled or target point reached) should be such that, if your opponent does not move, the point of your blade should be just past the back of his head and so, in real terms, your opponent will be dead. If your opponent moves back, then the strike can be extended slightly by increasing the length of pass with the back foot and/or flexing the forward knee.

If your opponent reacts, it is likely to be in one of three ways: To step back out of distance and enter into the bind; to present an equal and opposite challenge and endeavour to push you out of the centre whilst entering into the bind; or to threaten you from a different line. If he threatens from a different line, then you should already have adopted one of the other Maisterhaw in the Single Time. If he binds with your sword, at the moment of contact you must use Fühlen to discover if he is weak or strong in resistance. If he is weak, then extend forward to make a direct thrust along the eye-line to the face, half-stepping or even passing again, if necessary. If he is strong in the bind, perform the Schilhaw as described below, or be weak and pass around him. Your end position, after performing the perfect Zornhaw, will be the completed Zornort with the rear leg now forward. For the right-handed fencer this will be the right leg, for the left-handed fencer the left leg.

Zornhaw Notes

Position of the Krumphaw

2. The Krumphaw

[This is] the **Krumphaw**, together with techniques [to use with it].
Deliver a Krumphaw upwards quickly; throw your point at your opponent's hands.

Gloss.
This lesson teaches how you should deliver the Krumphaw to your opponent's hands. Also use this technique: if he strikes at the opening on your right side with an Oberhaw or an **Underhaw,** then step away from the blow with your right foot towards his left side, and with your arms extended strike his hands with your point. This technique can also be used if he faces you in the Ochs guard.

Expansion:
The Krumphaw, or 'crooked strike', removes a threat from an Oberhaw, or thrust in the upper line, and an Underhaw, both towards your right side, assuming you are right-handed. If your entry into the first True Time is threatened before you have managed to achieve the Zornhaw, then you must look to remove the threat, and this is done by controlling your opponent's weapon via his hands. This advantage is then improved by removing yourself from his centreline and creating a new one to his left side whilst simultaneously forcing him to maintain his original line. This is achieved by stepping onto the outside of his movement and is a 'moving the centreline' strike. You are safe from threat because you are cutting at the extended target with the tip of your blade and are consequently in the first True Time relative to his hands. Your opponent's target is your body, which is now at the second True Time relative to him, so as long as you have control of his hands at the wrist with the last 6" of your blade he cannot reach you. In this following example, we will assume that both parties are starting in a static guard and your opponent's position is the open Ochs, which for the right-handed is with the right foot forward, and your static position will be with the left foot forward, possibly in the Pflug. If you are a left-handed fencer, you will stand with your right foot forward and execute the strike as if mirroring the example described below.

The Krumphaw is executed as follows: Entry from the static guard should be achieved via the Zornort, where your weight must continue forward over the front foot in the manner described in the Zornhaw. If you sense a threat from your opponent on your right side (most likely a thrust to your face from his Ochs, but do NOT perform this against a dynamic opponent until you are comfortable with the movement and familiar with the True Times) then, as your back foot is coming forward, disengage your point from the centre in a clockwise circular motion (against and then away from his sword) and slightly extend to collect his hands at the wrist on the outside. By placing a slight force on the tip of your sword in towards the centre his wrist will continue to follow its previous line but, because your back foot is in transition, this will push your balance to his left side, so you must compensate by moving the transitional rear foot to that side in order to maintain balance. How far you need to step across is very much dependent on how strong your opponent is at the sword. If he gives way as a consequence of the displacement then you will not be pushed so far out from the centre. If he is strong at the sword, then you will be pushed further from the centre. In either case, it is important to ensure that your finished distance is in Time of Hand relative to your target, which in this instance is his forward wrist. When recovering with what is now the rear foot to secure the new centreline, the extra turning movement will cut your opponent's wrist and by bending the front knee and extending the reach (see '*Extending forward*', above) you must look to lift or roll his hands over his head (if caught in the high line) and push them off-balance, cutting the wrist as he overbalances and passing through with the foot again, if necessary. If he is in the low line, then if necessary, invert the blade to displace the threat away (tip pointing downward), and with a clockwise circular motion, cut with the short edge to the wrist, thus controlling the hands and preventing any return.

Whilst performing the Krumphaw do not extend the hands forward of the leading shoulder, but maintain a position in front of the chest. If you wish to push the hands forward, do so by rotating the shoulders and bending the front knee; to put the hands ahead of the shoulder is to be weak in the bind. The Krumphaw can be struck from either side with either foot forward, meaning with or against the orientation of your lower body.

Krumphaw Notes

Position of the Schilhaw

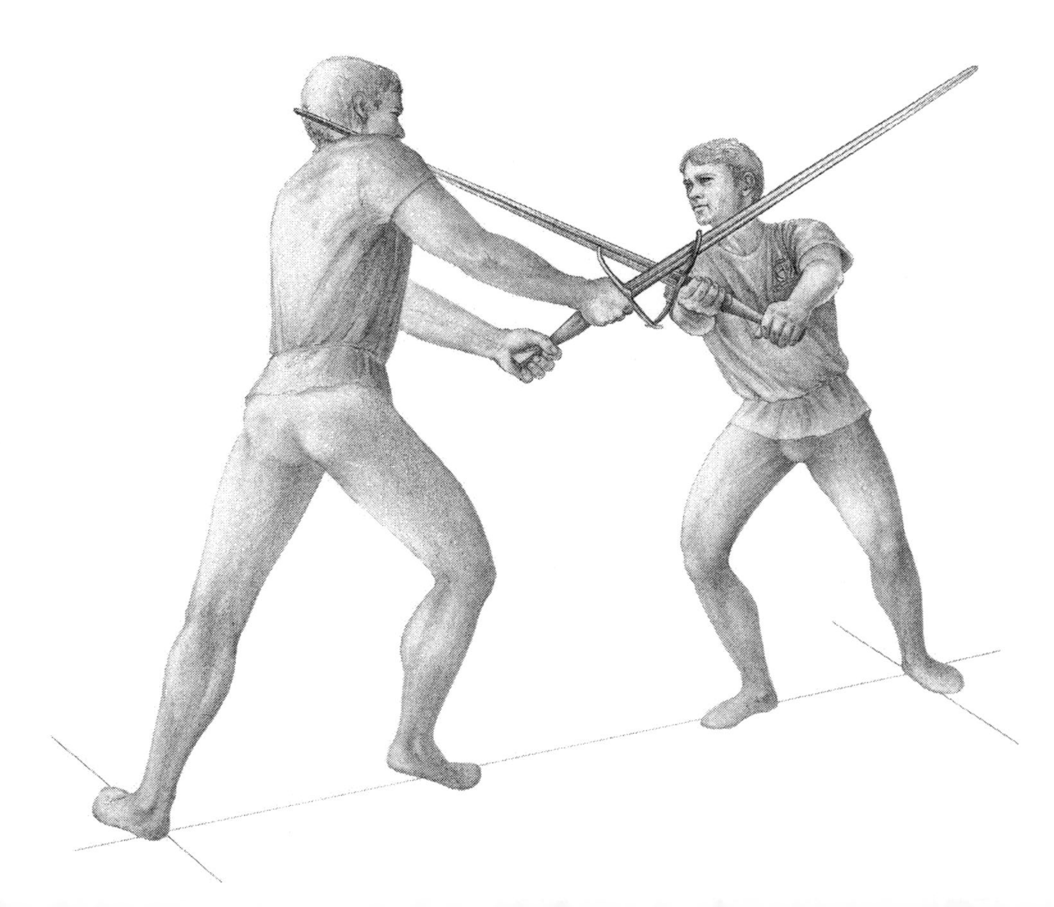

3. The Schilhaw (also called the Schiller)

[This is] the Schilhaw, and the techniques [to be used with it].
The Schiller breaks blows or thrusts from the ruffian. He who trusts in ***Wechsel****, will be robbed of his certainty by the Schiller.*

Gloss.
Note this: the Schiller is a blow that breaks the blows and thrusts from those ruffians who claim mastery [of the sword] by use of force. This is how the blow is to be struck: if your opponent strikes at you from his right side, you should strike from your right side with the short edge and with extended arms against his blow, striking the Schwech of his sword, and strike him on his right shoulder. If he attempts a Durch wechseln , make your blow into a long thrust into his chest. Use this strike also if your adversary opposes you in the Pflug guard or if he attempts to thrust at you below.

Expansion:
The Schilhaw, or as I call it 'the shield strike', is a useful tool in our repertoire. It allows us to engage against a threat in the low line whilst presenting a counter. Because of the nature of the body mechanics used in the Schilhaw, it presents a strong defence against those who ply their system with force. It is also a very effective counter to a thrust from the low line because of the nature by which the Schilhaw is engaged. The Schilhaw is a 'challenging the centreline' strike. In this example, we shall assume both parties are right-handed and starting from a static position with your opponent taking the Pflug on his right side. You are possibly in the Pflug on your right side with your left foot forward. If you are a left-handed fencer performing the Schilhaw, you will stand with your right foot forward.

The Schilhaw is executed as follows: Entry from the static guard should be achieved via the Zornort, where your weight must continue forward over the front foot and along the centreline in the manner described in the Zornhaw. Because this is a 'challenging the centreline' strike, your intent must be travelling along the shortest route between you and your opponent, this being the centreline. Keep extending forward and pass with the intention of performing a Zornhaw until you have reason to do otherwise. If you sense a threat to your left side, push your hands across to intercept by turning the shoulders, moving into the false grip whilst doing so. This movement will disengage your point from the centre and is necessary in order to guide the Schwech of your opponent's sword onto your Störck. The rotation of your sword into the false grip should not only collect his blade against your crossguard but also scribe a circle with your tip, in much the same way as the Zwerhaw. During this rotation, it allows you to accelerate the tip speed in order to effect a significant downward blow against his right shoulder with the short edge. If you feel your hands being lifted by your opponent, push your sword down and if you feel your hands being pushed down, raise yours to compensate. The ideal position you are looking for is the True Cross, where the pressure against your sword is perpendicular to that of your opponent.

The movement is a sweeping motion with your hands driven by the shoulders and performed with strong arms. It is this sweeping motion that collects a thrust along the low line. If you bend the arms at any point, your opponent will perform a counter Schilhaw, so it is imperative that strong arms are maintained throughout the movement and the point is such that you draw your opponent's Schwech onto your Störck. If your opponent attempts Durch wechseln , extend forward along the centreline and thrust into the chest, though if you have performed the Schilhaw properly, the Durch wechseln is unlikely to occur unless you have physically batted his sword away. The Schilhaw can be struck from either side with either foot forward, meaning with or against the orientation of your lower body.

Schilhaw Notes

Position of the Zwerhaw

4. The Zwerhaw (also called the Zwerch)

[This is] the Zwerhaw and the techniques [to use with it].
*The Zwerch masters [any blow] that comes from **Vom Tage**.*

Gloss.
Take note: the Zwerhaw breaks all blows that are struck from above downwards. This is how you should perform the blow: If your opponent strikes from above at your head, you should step away from the blow with your right foot towards his left side. And as you step, turn your sword with the hilt high in front of your head, so that your thumbs are downwards, and strike his left side with the short edge. In this way you will catch his blow with your hilt and will strike him on the head.

Expansion:
The Zwerhaw, or as we refer to it to aid memory the 'helicopter of death', is a very versatile and strong strike. As Ringeck has already said, it will protect your head from any downward strike aimed at you from above whilst simultaneously presenting a counter. It works in much the same way as the Krumphaw, by moving your centreline whist maintaining your opponent's original line of intent, making this a 'moving the centreline' strike. Where this differs from the Krumphaw is that you are collecting his strike with the Störck of your blade whilst simultaneously striking the head. In this example we shall assume that both parties are right-handed, starting from a static position with your opponent taking the Vom Tage on his right side and your static position will be with the left foot forward, possibly in the Pflug. If you are a left-handed fencer performing the Zwerhaw, you will stand with your right foot forward.

The Zwerhaw is executed as follows: Entry from the static guard should be achieved via the Zornort, where your weight must continue forward over the front foot and along the centreline in the manner described above in the Zornhaw. If you sense a threat coming from above, raise the hands towards that threat, starting the change into the false grip in order to make contact on the inside of his blade with yours. Because your back foot is in transition, you will experience a weight-shift to your right side because the effort required to collect your opponent's sword will cause you to start turning your shoulders towards the threat and so throw your body mass in the opposite direction. This change in direction of momentum, from linear to rotational, causes your point of balance to be thrown forward and to your right side, resulting in the passing foot, in this case the right foot, moving diagonally towards his left side in order to maintain balance. You need to ensure that your diagonal step, combined with him coming forward along the original line, will put you a sword's length away from the back of his head, along the centreline, and no more than an arm's length away from his centre. This means that, because you have already collected his sword, the rotational movement of the hands rising, combined with moving into false grip, should have caused your opponent's blade to be at your Störck and your hands still on his centreline. You could view it as pushing yourself out of his centreline and as the transitional foot finds its appropriate place towards his left side, so your left foot must now pass across and become the back foot on your new centreline. This pass across with the left foot brings with it an extra turn of the shoulders and hips, raising the hands above your head to complete the strike with a near horizontal cut to the head/neck, the final cut finishing when the back foot finds its place on the new centreline.

It is important that you DO NOT remove yourself from the original centreline too soon. If this should happen, your opponent will follow your movement out of his centre with his pass sooner than you can collect his blade, since it is this contact with his blade that keeps him on his original line. It is also important that the arms remain strong from the point of entry with the Zornort to the finish, the final cut being achieved with the back foot coming around and so drawing the edge home with the strength of the shoulders and hips and not the arms. When collecting the threat, your point should shoot forward to make contact with the left side of his sword as quickly as possible, starting the turn into the false grip during this movement and drawing him onto your Störck. As the hands continue upward to collect his blade on the Störck of yours, so your tip scribes a natural circle around the head of your opponent, transferring its position from the right side of his head to the left side. All the time this circle is scribed, the tip speed increases and the resultant contact on the other side of his neck has significant power, because the movement is driven by the shoulders and hips and, in turn, from the feet. The Zwerhaw is a foot-dependent strike and can only be completed when the upper body, hips and feet are in the same orientation, unlike the Krumphaw.

Zwerhaw Notes

Position of the Schaytler

5. The Schaytler (also spelled schaittler)

[This describes] the Schaytler and the techniques to be used with it.
The Schaytler endangers the face.

Gloss:
Note this: the Schaytler is a danger to the face and the chest. It should be used in this manner: if your opponent faces you in the Alber guard, you should strike a Schaytler with the long edge downwards from above from a distance. Keep your arms high, and hang your point in to his face.

Expansion:
The Schaytler, or 'parting strike', specifically breaks the Alber and involves the most complicated movement of all the Maisterhaw, so consequently being the most difficult to explain. Although the principle methodology is consistent with the philosophy of the system, there are several possible actions to a reaction from your opponent relative to your threat, so when we enter with the Schaytler, it is with the sole intention of presenting a sufficient threat to force a reaction. It is also the only Maisterhaw predominantly entered into distance with a pass from the back foot as opposed to a half-step with the front foot, and does not rely on the Zornort to gain entry into the second True Time. There are several different possible outcomes from one entry and each one is an offshoot from the other.

The initial intention is to strike to the top of your opponent's head from the Schaytler position. Because of the nature of the Alber, this intention needs to lead with the point, keeping the hands very high and out of reach from the upper cut from the Alber for as long as possible. If this target is out of reach and your opponent has not reacted to you, then continue down to threaten the face, chest and subsequently hands, in that order, looking to effect a cut on each as you descend whilst still leading with the point. Because of the speed at which this entry is performed, if your opponent still has not reacted and no target strike has been achieved, you move to the final position for this stage, which is with the sword point at the floor, crossing your opponent's blade with your hands in the false grip. Your intention is to force your opponent to follow one predictable line of cut, which you then counter by following up and thrusting into the lower line from the upper quarter. You must react as a consequence of your opponent and not in spite of him.

Entry: The ideal static starting point for the Schaytler is the second position of the Vom Tage, as described in 'The Four Guards' below, with the left foot forward and the point of your sword high and forward, with your hands above your head, so threatening your opponent along the centreline from above. We are assuming both you and your opponent are right-handed. At the point of entry, you raise your hands in an arc, pushing the point down and the hands up in order to threaten your opponent from above in a downward motion with the tip. Simultaneously, the back shoulder comes forward followed by the hip and then a pass with the back foot, along the centre.

There are several points to remember at this juncture:

i) Show full intent on entry, but do not be over-committed with the pass, as there is a good likelihood that your opponent will raise his point in an endeavour to cut at the extended target. This is why you must keep your hands above the point.
ii) You are cutting with the long edge, so the shoulders will be square with the centreline on entry.
iii) You are endeavouring to threaten the top of your opponent's head. Should he lean back or be out of distance, then you must look to threaten the face and subsequently the chest as you push the point down.

This is the Schaytler. Everything from this point will be 'from the Schaytler' and the possible avenues of response diverge, depending on the action of your opponent.

Passive opponent:
If your opponent does nothing but avoid the threat, then you must keep pushing the point down as you pass through with the back foot. Look to cut the face, chest and then the hands/extended target, before reaching the final position of point forward (to the floor and covering your opponent's blade), hands on the outside of the forward leg (most likely in the false grip and over your right knee) with your right foot forward and both knees slightly bent. If you have missed all the target points, you will be at the outer limits of the second True Time and possibly be entering into the third. It will seem that you

are off-balance with your feet in one orientation and your shoulders in the opposite one, the beauty of this particular technique now comes to the fore. Because you are looking to be in the first True Time, you have set yourself up for the next pass when, bringing the left foot forward, you will uncoil, bringing your feet and hips in line with your shoulders and into a strong position. You are trying to limit your opponent's strike path to one that is totally predictable to you, so he cannot achieve a strike unless he first cuts around your sword to your right side. By also adopting this position, you are denying your opponent the opportunity to cut your lower leg/knee, as your covering sword will not allow it.

It is from this point that other possibilities may occur:

1) One possible scenario is that your opponent will not move and so a stalemate occurs. Staying true to the system, you must not let this happen but continue with your attack. Here are two possible actions relative to your likely situation:-

    a) If you have carried no forward momentum through, then the continued attack can be looking to stab the foot as you finish this movement from the Schaytler and force your opponent to break his position.
    b) If you have carried momentum through, then keeping the sword/hand position as you pass through with the foot again, look to wrestle with your opponent using one of the Ringen techniques, covered in a later grade.

2) Another possibility is that your opponent cuts around your sword and to your right side. As he starts cutting, you must immediately perform a deep pass through with the back foot, bringing the hips and feet in line with the shoulders as you do so, and pushing your hands out to collect his blade on your Störck. Keep the point below the hands and lift your sword behind his; 'because of him' rather than 'despite him'. By that, I mean you follow his raise, not force it, because if you do force the lift, then your Schwech will slide to his Störck and you will be countered with a thrust from below. Your opponent may respond in one of two ways:-

a) If he continues to lift higher to escape your Störck, then as you lift to maintain the contact, look for a thrust into the lower opening as your point aligns with it.
b) If he stops lifting his hands, then maintaining his sword on your Störck, push down with the hands and lift the point, so thrusting into an upper opening in a process not too dissimilar to the Schilhaw.

It is important that the pass through with the back foot is deep into the first True Time as you are trying to enter inside the opponent's point. Not to be committed will endanger your advantage, but over-commitment will undermine your intent, so be vigilant with regards to distance and ensure that you control the centre at all times. This last play (see 2, above) accommodates any cut by your opponent from the point where the Schaytler ends and you reach the beginning of the first play (see 1, above). As he moves, you must instantly look to pass through with the back foot and intercept his sword, as described in the last play (2), searching for openings in which to thrust and moving your hands in order to achieve and maintain the Störck. If you find yourself out of position for a thrust, or your opponent steps in as you do, then use the (1b) option above and look to Ringen or a disarm. This is the Art and it requires knowledge of the principles 'Fühlen' and 'In des' in order to execute it properly (which will be covered in a later grade). At this time, concentrate on the movement, balance and distance.

It is highly unlikely that this end play will occur as the Alber relies on a fast upper cut to the extended target, which will be your hands. By leading with the point downward from the Schaytler and along the centreline, so keeping the hand higher than your point, your opponent runs the risk of skewering his own hands upon your point before achieving his target, so he will have to strike around your sword to prevent this, giving you more time to react. Also, given the nature of the Alber, the direction in which he strikes around will most likely be towards your right side, if he is right-handed, so allowing more opportunity for you to react appropriately. If your opponent is actively cutting up during your execution of the initial Schaytler, then the next section describes your reaction.

Active opponent:
An active opponent will attempt to cut early to your hands during your initial entry with the Schaytler. If you have entered properly, your back foot will be passing through as you do so and you will be coming forward but not be over-committed. As you see his sword lift, which is usually a result of him leaning back to avoid the cut to the head/face, immediately stop your forward movement by stamping the passing foot into the ground in front of you. At the same time, pull the pommel hand sharply back onto your left side by turning the shoulders, thus entering into the open Ochs, keeping the forward elbow tucked into the body and the wrist well back. All things being correct, your opponent's tip should pass upward, missing you and your hands, and because of the snatching nature of an upward strike executed from the Alber, the momentum will cause him to continue upward, past the line of your Ochs, at which point you must come forward again with a thrust along his eye-line by extending forward. This will result in one of two possibilities:-

i) You will drive your tip through the eye of your opponent
ii) Your opponent will continue lifting into the **Krone,** in order to displace your thrust up and over his head.

Should the latter occur, then you must drop your hands below those of your opponent, sliding your blade from his crossguard and onto his wrists, and stepping through, roll his hands over his head with the Schwech of your sword, preferably the last 6 inches. Your sword, being sharp, will either cut through his wrist if he resists or allow you to push him off-balance and so finish the cut by drawing through the wrist as he tries to recover. This final movement is not dissimilar to the end of the Krumphaw. If your opponent is being particularly difficult, as you lift his hands, you can push your crossguard into his face to force the head back and him off balance.

If your opponent's tip does not pass beyond your hands, because you pulled into the Ochs too early or he perceived your action so did not over commit, then immediately reach across to engage his Schwech on your Störck, and pushing his threat out to your right side, stepping in deep and to your left whilst doing so, start the entry into the action described in Passive Opponent (2).

It is important that, as a student, you have a certain level of familiarity and competence with a sword before a complex strike like the Schaytler can be performed with relative success. Knowledge of time, distance and the ability to perceive the intention of your opponent is paramount to getting the Schaytler, and the options that stem from it, correct more often than not. Saying this, performing a strike from the Schaytler is still a risky option against an opponent who understands the versatility of the Alber, which is why any entry against the Alber must be made decisively and with commitment. Not to threaten your opponent with the initial entry is, quite literally, playing into his hands!

As mentioned before, the Schaytler is the most difficult strike to perfect and is one of the last items we teach a student trying to achieve Grade 2. We tend to grade in favour of a Grade 2 candidate who shows an understanding of the movement and principles involved with respect to the Schaytler, rather than performing it perfectly in every situation. We expect a student to have perfected the Schaytler and all its nuances by the end of Grade 3, which is included in the next publication.

Schaytler Notes

The Four Guards

These are the four guards.
Hold fast to the four guards alone, and shun the others. Ochs, Pflug, Alber and Vom Tag should not be unknown to you.

Gloss.
This means that you should use no guard except one of the four that have been named here.

Expansion:
The four guards consist of the Ochs, Pflug, Vom Tage, and Alber, and are explained below. Each guard position protects one of the four openings and these are also explained below. Be aware that any static guard should be taken beyond the second True Time of your opponent, so in his Time of the hand, body and foot, or feet, and to take a static guard closer than this, and not be in the bind, is reckless and foolhardy. Knowing the True Times, and how they relate to distance and intent, is fundamental to the Art, so study the four guards and understand them in this context. Take note of hand position, balance, posture, foot position and control, as these are the elements that define the guards and show us why Liechtenauer recommends them as the only positions you will need to know. Each guard has strengths and weaknesses over the others and it is vital that you understand what these characteristics are so that you are prepared, thus taking the appropriate guard position to oppose that of your opponent during the initial confrontation. These elements, and many more, are expanded further within the chapter 'Conclusion' at the end of the manual.

The position of the Ochs

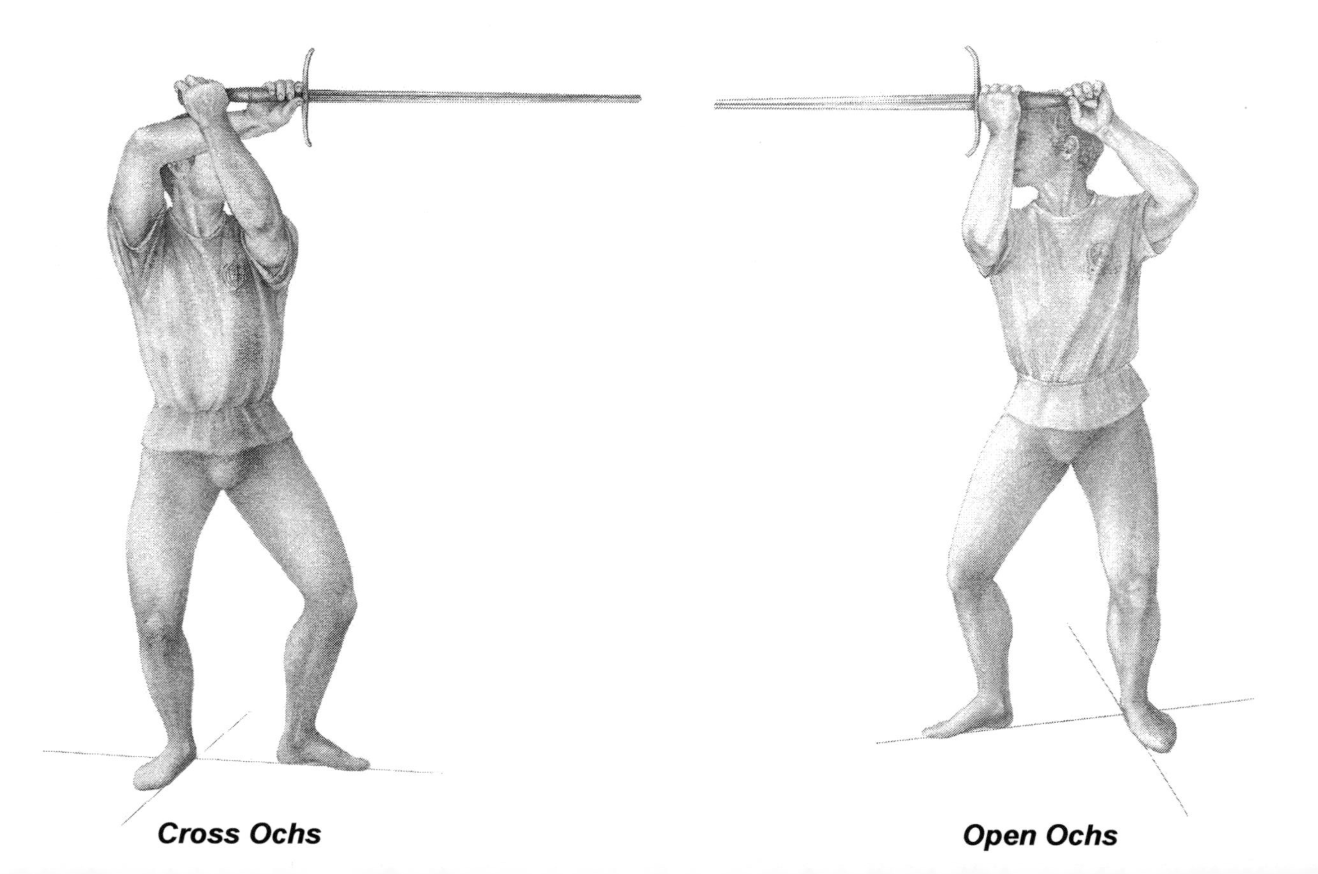

1. The Ochs

The Ochs. Place yourself as directed: stand with the left foot forwards and hold your sword next to your right side in front of your head, and let your point hang towards your opponent's face.

Expansion:
As Ringeck suggests, the Ochs or 'ox' is a high guard because the hands are above the waist, so anyone standing in it will be 'claiming the centreline'. It is a threat to your opponent's face and surprisingly difficult to see when done properly, so it is important that you maintain the line of the blade along the line of your opponent's eyesight, so all he can see is your crossguard and hands and not the blade itself, denying him the perception of distance relative to your point.

The proper position for the Ochs, as described by Ringeck and assuming you are right-handed, is what we refer to as the cross Ochs, because the arms are crossed. It is as follows: You must have your right hand in the foregrip and left on the pommel grip of the sword. With your feet a shoulder's width apart, stand with your left foot forward aligned with the centreline, pointing at your opponent. The right foot is behind, with the heel also on the centreline, its alignment perpendicular to the centreline with the foot pointing outwards. Knees should be slightly flexed and in a comfortable position with the hips and shoulders bladed (in line with the centreline) and the left side facing your opponent. Your centre of gravity should be above the centreline, and your weight should be evenly distributed between the forward and back foot. The upper left arm should be perpendicular to the centreline and horizontal, with the left hand gripping the pommel. The upper right arm should also be close to horizontal with the right forearm crossing the inside of the left and the right hand above the left elbow, loosely gripping the foregrip position on the handle. Align the blade along the eye-line of your opponent so he is looking directly along the length of the sword and cannot focus on anything other than your crossguard. DO NOT allow your forward elbow to protrude in front of the shoulder, otherwise your opponent will treat it as an extended target. In this orientation, movement is achieved by pivoting from the pommel hand and steering with the forehand, so the mass of the sword is being held by the pommel hand, making any movement from the forehand firm, quick and accurate. This is the cross Ochs for the right-handed fencer. For the left-handed fencer, the cross Ochs is exactly the same but mirrored, i.e. left hand on the foregrip and right foot forward along the centreline.

The Ochs from the other side, with the right foot and the right hand forward, is what we refer to as the open Ochs because your arms are not crossed. It is as follows: With your feet a shoulder's width apart, stand with your right foot forward, aligned with the centreline, pointing at your opponent. As before, the rear foot, in this case the left, has its heel on the centreline with the foot pointing outwards, perpendicular to the centreline. The knees should be slightly flexed and in a comfortable position with the hips and shoulders bladed, the right side facing your opponent. Your weight should be evenly distributed between the forward and back foot. The upper right arm should be perpendicular to the centreline and horizontal, with the forehand holding the foregrip position. The upper left arm should be close to horizontal, with the left hand lightly gripping the pommel. As before, align the blade along the eye-line of your opponent and keep the forward elbow tucked in line with the shoulder. Again, control of the blade is achieved by supporting and pivoting the sword from the forward shoulder, in this case the right via the right hand, and steering with the rear shoulder, in this case the left via the left hand, thus allowing a firm, quick and accurate movement of the tip. This is the open Ochs for the right-handed fencer. For the left-handed fencer, the open Ochs is exactly the same but mirrored, i.e. left hand on the foregrip and left foot forward along the centreline.

From the Ochs you can threaten all four openings of your opponent but to challenge any other than the upper openings will require significant movement and almost certainly put you in the Nach. Considering the manner by which the guard is adopted, placing a forward threat in the upper line and along your opponent's eye-line, the most efficient entry will be a thrust along that line and into the face, though I recommend that any entry from the Ochs is performed with diligence and care to your training partner's safety. When using intent, masks must be worn and consideration exercised.

You can also easily defend the upper and lower openings, though the technique used to do so needs to be practised and used in the proper time with the body and foot during the execution of a counter-movement. As for counter guards, the Ochs presents a formidable threat to the upper line and so is suitable to oppose any of the guards except the Alber, or a threat from below that predominantly favours the extended target.

Striking from Ochs:
The dynamic of the Ochs is not favourably inclined towards striking quickly, but more involves thrusting and displacement within the Wind thus, striking is usually achieved when shedding a threat, and presenting a counter whilst stepping. Here is a useful exercise to increase understanding of the Ochs and countering from it. This exercise should be performed from both sides.

Stand in either Ochs as described above. The movement starts with pivoting the sword within the forehand. By pushing forward and up with the pommel the flat of the blade will rest downward along the outside of the forearm, supporting the blade on the outside of the elbow. Keeping the sword in this orientation (i.e. vertically downward), rotate the arms above the head in order to lay the blade along the middle of the back. At this point, pass through with the foot along the centreline in order to change sides, maintaining the orientation and position of the sword blade down the back. When the step has been completed, continue the rotational movement of the hands, with the blade still vertically down, onto the now forward elbow, so you have effectively travelled in a circle and are now in the start position as before but on the opposite side. Extend forward by bending the front knee and cutting from below with the long edge, drawing back into the Ochs by pulling the pommel back. You will notice that the Ochs is now on the opposite side to your starting position. From here you reverse the process back to the Ochs on the original side. The passing through with the foot can either be forwards or backwards, and it is important that you practise the movement in both directions. We will expand on this exercise in the next book, to provide a useful drill between two students.

Ochs Notes

Ochs Notes

The position of the Pflug

2. The Pflug

The Pflug. Place yourself as directed: stand with the left foot forwards and hold your sword with crossed hands next to your right side above your knee, so that your point is towards your opponent's face.

Expansion:
The Pflug, or 'plough', is held with the hands below the waist, making it a 'challenging the centreline' guard and it provides a low line position of offence with adequate time to manoeuvre into any alternative posture. Because of the low hand position and the blade being held along the eye-line towards your opponent, which can distract him from looking at you and concentrating on trying to perceive the threat from the blade, the Pflug provides a good and comfortable static position from which to effect an entry. It is also the most convenient guard from which to enter into the Zornort. You should favour this guard as a starting point for entering into the Maisterhaw, as it provides an immediate yet non-visible threat from the point of entry onwards and it can offer a distraction to the inexperienced or unnerve even the more experienced opponent. In either situation, it can offer you an advantage and so provide the means by which to succeed.

The Pflug, assuming you are a right-handed fencer, is held with the right hand in the foregrip and left hand on the pommel grip. As a consequence of this particular guard position having the arms crossed, we refer to it as the cross Pflug. You stand with the left foot forward and your body bladed with the left side towards your opponent, so your shoulders are as close to in line with the centreline as possible. You must be in a relaxed, upright stance with your centre of gravity above the centreline, your weight evenly distributed between both feet, both knees slightly flexed and your feet a shoulder's width apart. Your heels should be along the centreline, the forward foot pointing towards your opponent and the back foot perpendicular to the centreline. You should stand with the hands in a light grip close to the body, in line with the hip in the lower position (arms extended) with the pommel hand above the rear knee (in this case the right). Your hands will be behind the centre of the body, thus removing any extended target, with the forearms crossed and the forehand outside, pommel hand inside, with the blade towards and along the eye-line of your opponent. This way your opponent is looking onto the tip, directly down the length of your blade, and so this will disappear from his view. Your arms need to be relaxed with the elbows slightly bent and your general demeanour must portray calm and control, as if you are literally in a stance that you could maintain all day if needs be. This is the cross Pflug and it should be taken in this manner by a right-handed fencer. For the left-handed fencer, this guard is exactly the same but mirrored, i.e. left hand on the foregrip and right foot/hip/shoulder towards your opponent and along the centreline.

The Pflug can be taken with the right hand in the foregrip and the right foot forward also. We refer to this as the open Pflug because the arms are not crossed. Stand with your feet a shoulder's width apart, heels on the centreline, the forward foot (in this case the right) pointing towards your opponent and along the centreline, with the back foot perpendicular to it. Your knees should be slightly bent with the centre of gravity over the centreline and weight evenly distributed between both feet. With a light grip on the sword handle, your hands should be close to the body, in line with the hip with the pommel hand above the rear knee (in this case the left), holding the blade forward the along the eye-line of your opponent, so removing any extended target. Your arms should be relaxed with the elbows slightly bent and the forearms uncrossed. This is the open Pflug and it should be taken in this manner by a right-handed fencer. For the left-handed fencer, this guard is exactly the same but mirrored, i.e. left hand on the foregrip and left foot/hip/shoulder towards your opponent with the hands gripping the pommel over the right knee.

Striking from Pflug

The Pflug can threaten all of the four openings of your opponent, using a thrust from the lower line, with the most effective entry from the Pflug being the Schilhaw. If your opponent has no regard for his own safety and does not recognise the threat that the Pflug presents, then as he enters into distance, so enter also and direct your thrust upward along the centreline and into the chin/neck, finishing in the Zornort while passing through with the foot. Not only will you gain the Vor by entering in this manner, but if your opponent does nothing you will, if using a simulator (shinai or similar) and you are both properly protected, lift his chin and flip your opponent from his feet and onto his back. This alone could result in a serious injury, so the full force thrust must be moderated according to the simulator used, protection worn and experience acquired, avoiding at all costs the possibility of injury to your opponent and yourself. In reality, you would drive your sword through his skull from below, most likely killing him or at least controlling his balance, but as this is theoretical and NOT what we are trying to achieve, consideration MUST be shown.

When striking a wide, open blow from the static Pflug guard, you spend a considerable amount of time moving into the strike and give your opponent every opportunity to take the Vor, thus rendering your strike useless. If you do displace your tip from the centreline, then do so as a consequence of your opponent's action rather than despite it, and whilst passing forward through the Zornort. Should you need to displace a threat, then counter simultaneously using the Schilhaw or move into one of the other Maisterhaw.

The Pflug is a versatile guard and it gives you a good opportunity to enter with relative confidence as all of the Maisterhaw flow from it, through the Zornort, with ease. It also allows you to defend your four openings with the advantage of being able to present a counter threat in most cases.

Pflug Notes

Pflug Notes

The position of Vom Tage

Over-head hand position

3. The Vom Tage

The Vom Tage. Place yourself as directed: stand with your left foot forwards and hold your sword by your right shoulder, or hold it with extended arms above your head.

Expansion:
The Vom Tage, or 'from the sky', is held with the hands above the waistline, so making it a 'claiming the centreline' guard. The blade, held above the eye-line, makes the threat of an Oberhaw to the top of your opponent's head obvious, hence the name 'from the sky'. To take this guard means you are making a statement of authority and claiming a dominant position, but it also has the reverse effect of committing you to the centreline, so any strike from it must be committed. Having the point away from the centre, with little to hit other than the head of your opponent in Single Time, does limit the versatility of the Vom Tage, but having your extended target away from your opponent's reach gives you a major advantage with regards to intended threat. If you were to strike the Schaytler it would be from the Vom Tage guard with the hands held extended above your head.

To take the guard of the Vom Tage, assuming you are right-handed, you must have your right hand in the foregrip position, your left hand on the pommel grip and your left foot towards your opponent. The feet will be a shoulder's width apart with both heels on the centreline, the forward foot pointing towards your opponent along the centreline with the rear foot perpendicular to it, pointing outwards. Your knees should be slightly bent with your body weight distributed evenly between both feet. You should be in an upright position, with your back straight and head up, as if standing to attention, with the side adjacent to the forward foot (in this case your left side) bladed towards your opponent. The forward arm will be tucked close against the body, thus removing any extended target, with the pommel hand pushed into the rear shoulder. The sword will be pointing directly upward, with the foregrip in line with the ear, rearmost forearm (right) perpendicular to the sword, parallel with the floor, with the elbow high, in much the same position as if pulling a longbow string. Your face will be towards your opponent and your general demeanour should be one of calm and control. This is the Vom Tage and it should be taken in this manner by a right-handed fencer. To take this guard if you are left-handed, then mirror this position by standing with your right foot forward whilst having the left hand on the foregrip and the right hand on the pommel grip of the sword handle.

The Vom Tage can also be taken with the hands back, high above your head, blade tilted forward towards the top of the head of your opponent. This is the position from which the Schaytler starts and although it can be taken with the left foot forward, as in the Schaytler, it is specific to a Vom Tage taken with the opposite foot forward. To take this guard, for a right-handed fencer, stand with the right hand in the foregrip position and with either foot forward. The heels should be on the centreline and a shoulder's width apart, the forward foot pointing along the centreline towards your opponent and the rear foot perpendicular to the centreline and pointing out. Knees should be slightly bent but the centre of balance must be fractionally forward, ready to fall upon your opponent, but not so far forward that the option of drawing back is inhibited. The hips need to move fluidly in order to allow the shoulders to be square to the centreline but remember that the shoulder should never be in front of the forward knee. The arms should be raised high over the head with the hands above the shoulders, elbows slightly bent and pushed outwards in order to achieve this comfortably and to avoid offering an extended target to your opponent. The hands should grip the sword handle lightly but securely, allowing the blade to lean slightly forward and so threatening your opponent's head from above. When taking this guard, especially against the Alber, it is important to be on the outskirts of the third True Time, the forward balance bringing your upper body closer to, but not into, the second True Time.

Striking from Vom Tage

The Vom Tage, although offering the potential of striking to any of the four openings, with regards to presenting a threat in Single Time can only realistically threaten with a strike from above, and it is with this threat that an opponent must be controlled. Because of this, your opponent is unlikely to strike towards a lower opening because all that you need do is step back with the forward foot, whilst simultaneously reaching forward to strike the top of his head, keeping your lower body in the third True Time, thus drawing him immediately into a defensive position and giving you the Vor. Be careful not to be drawn out, so you then have your hands cut with a strike to your extended target as with the Krumphaw, or to be engaged, side-stepped and cut to the head as in the Zwerhaw.

Striking from the first position of the Vom Tage, with the right hand in the foregrip, left foot forward and pommel hand into the shoulder, initiate the strike by punching forward with the right hand, so taking the Vor. It is important to have the right forearm parallel with the ground in order that the initial movement, when punching through, presents an immediate threat. To allow the elbow to drop will cause the strike to lift before presenting a threat, thus giving time to your opponent and so the opportunity to gain the Vor. After the hands have initiated the movement of punching forward, straightening the arms whilst doing so, it is important that the shoulders turn into the strike, driving the body through with the right shoulder, followed by the hips and the straightening of the front leg, completing the movement as the back foot passes through along the centreline. If practising the strike without an opponent, you should pass into the Zornort, giving you the option of entering into any of the Maisterhaw.

If striking from the second position of the Vom Tage, follow the movement as explained in the Schaytler. Never lead the blade with the hands from this position, as you offer an extended target to your opponent if you do so. It is important that you drive downward, keeping the tip of the blade below the hand, only changing to the hands leading when they drop below the shoulder line. If your opponent has not given you cause to diverge from the strike by this point, then it is usually safe to enter into the Zornort and the Maisterhaw. If your opponent's intent is from below, keep driving the point down as described in the Schaytler.

It is possible to defend all four openings from the Vom Tage with a combination of passing back and presenting a counter-threat from above or cutting into the strike and then entering into one of the four Maisterhaw although, because the Vom Tage is a 'claiming the centreline' guard, it is customary to take advantage of the threat from above and to strike quickly thus claiming the Vor.

Vom Tage Notes

Vom Tage Notes

The position of the Alber

4. The Alber

The Alber. Place yourself as directed: stand with your right foot forward and hold your sword with extended arms in front of you with the point on the ground.

Expansion:
The Alber, or 'fool' (either because you are a fool to use it or a fool to enter against it), is held with the hands below the waist so making it a 'challenging the centreline' guard. The Alber is an unusual position which, to the inexperienced fencer, appears very vulnerable as you are offering your head in exchange for a short edge Underhaw. The more experienced fencer will understand that the offer of a head strike is the bait, and as the user of the Alber, you are looking to hit the extended target (the forearms or hands), so you generally stay in the third True Time and out of range for his strike. The static Alber is taken with the right foot forward (with respect to a right-handed fencer) and is the only guard to represent a post- strike position, so making the Alber a post-strike guard. We call it 'post-strike' because having struck an Oberhaw from the right shoulder (passing through with the right foot, as is proper) continuing through until the point is placed on the floor, the Alber represents your finishing stance. The Alber is the only guard in the four recommended by Liechtenauer to represent a 'post-strike' position.

For the right-handed fencer to take the guard of the Alber, you must have the right hand on the foregrip and the right foot forward. The feet should be a stride's width apart (as if you were taking a good step) with the heel of each foot on the centreline, the forward foot pointing towards your opponent and the back foot (in this instance the left) perpendicular to the centreline, pointing outward. The weight should be slightly biased towards the front foot with the front knee bent, the back leg almost straight and a straight line formed between the back foot, hip and shoulder respectively. The shoulders should be at approximately 45° to the centreline and the arms straight but relaxed and extended, with the forehand in line with the front knee. The sword blade should be forward and towards the ground with the tip resting on the floor to your opponent's right side and approximately parallel with the centreline, though this element can be variable. Generally, the tip should not be so far from the centreline as to make an Underhaw into the centre difficult. For the left-handed fencer to take the guard of the Alber, you mirror this position with the left hand on the foregrip and the left foot forward.

As we have already mentioned, the static guard of the Alber should not be taken with the left foot forward if you are right-handed, and vice versa. The static guard position very much relies upon the extra reach achieved by having the forehand and respective foot in front giving you a Single Time cut from the post-strike position before a threat to the head, and the need to move, becomes pressing. To take the Alber with the opposing foot (to the forehand) in front puts you at a disadvantage, the most obvious one being to find yourself in the cross hand position in a Single Time cut as a consequence of having the opposite foot forward. Because of the nature of striking from the Alber, you cannot pass through with the foot quickly enough for the cross hand position to become open handed and still remain in Single Time so you will find yourself off-balance, out of time and consequently out of position. From a dynamic viewpoint, you are very unlikely ever to find yourself passing through a position where the opposite Alber occurs. A short edge Underhaw from a cross hand dynamic entry is weak, difficult to control and is why you are more likely either to be pulling back into the Pflug, applying one of the other Maisterhaw, or to be passing through whilst cutting upward from below with an open handed, long edge Underhaw into the open Ochs.

Striking from Alber:

Striking upward with the short edge from the open hand Alber is a straightforward action though, as we have already mentioned, the timing of that action is of great importance. Strike too early and your opponent will perceive your intent; strike too late and you will be hit. Your opponent will usually be attempting an Oberhaw of some description so, standing in the Alber as described above, look to cut to the extended target with the tip of your blade. The process by which this is achieved starts with the intention of your opponent. As he strikes the Oberhaw to your head, wait until the strike becomes a physical threat and start to lean back to avoid the cut, thus maintaining the third True Time relative to your opponent's target. Do not remove his target too quickly as this will result in your opponent abandoning his cause and changing his intent, but be ready to pass back with the forward foot by bending the rear leg and straightening the forward leg respectively. This action of drawing back will cause you to start lifting your tip, so continue this movement with a combination of lifting the arms and levering the forehand back with the shoulder, as a consequence of turning the shoulders square to the centreline and turning the hips with the passing back. Resist the temptation to lift the arms too high as your intention is to cut your opponent's wrist with the short edge tip of the blade and not to block the strike, since you should already be out of distance with the leaning and passing back.

Because the right hand, right foot and blade are already forward, you have removed the need to pass for the Single Time attack, relying on your opponent to enter into distance to achieve the short edge Underhaw. However, as your opponent will be looking to enter into the second True Time before he can effect his attack, you must be looking to pass back and maintain his Time of hand, body and foot. Although, from the static position, you are in the third True Time relative to your opponent's body, you are aiming for the extended target so your intention will be one time less, so in the second True Time relative to your opponent's forearms/hands. As you are also leaning forward and have extended your arms, your actual intent will be in the first True Time relative to your target. If your opponent does not instigate an entry, then you have the option to step in deep, close to his right side, by passing through with the back foot or by passing across with the front foot to your right side and engaging in one of the Maisterhaw, most likely the Krumphaw or Zwerhaw, or applying whichever technique will gain the advantage.

It is surprising to people just how quickly you can strike from the Alber and the huge variation of strikes you can implement from it. You might believe that there is only the opportunity for the short edge Underhaw into the lower right quarter of your opponent, and this is indeed the most obvious and quickest strike, but in reality you can cut or thrust into any of the four openings with relative ease, and it is this speed and versatility that makes the Alber so lethal. If you consider the distance the point has to travel in order to make contact with the extended target, and the fact that its mass is neutral by starting from a rested position on the floor, it is easy to see why the strike is so quick. As your reaction is dictated by the movement of your opponent striking at your head, you are already leaning back in order to avoid the strike and so naturally priming the lifting of the point; even if you do have to instigate the attack, you are close enough to prevent your opponent an opportunity to counter, so putting you in the Vor. When used against an inexperienced fencer you can almost guarantee a hit to the extended target, as your opponent's naivety will make him impatient to strike for the head from above with extended hands, so leaving him exposed to the deadly Alber from below.

Alber Notes

Alber Notes

The four guards:

Conclusive expansion

Remember that the guard positions should be taken beyond the second True Time and specifically with one foot forward according to which hand is on the foregrip (right-handed stand with the left foot forward, and vice versa). The reason for this is simple; in order to start the encounter, be it either in the Vor (you start the entry into distance with a half-step through into the Zornort, so leading the attack) or in the Nach (your opponent has entered into distance so leaving you to regain the advantage), you will have to take a pass either forwards (as with the Vor) or backwards (as possibly with the Nach) depending on your predicament and intent at that moment. This pass automatically puts you into a position of strength with the arms uncrossed and the correct foot forward (forehand and adjacent foot forward), so striking properly from your weak to your strong side. The guard positions are inherently weak and not intended for engagement, hence why they are in the third True Time, but in order to gain a passive, tactical advantage prior to engagement. This follows with the advice given in the 'text of the Second Lesson' within the 'General Advice' section at the beginning of 'The Exposition of the Manual' above.

The exception to this is the Alber which is taking a threatening position from below. The reason for this is that this guard, during the course of an encounter, would normally have been achieved after an Oberhaw (strike from above) had been made, so it is a post-strike guard. If you have struck through from your right side with an Oberhaw, and your opponent has leapt backward out of distance, you have the Alber as a recovery option as it is the best guard for a Single Time attack (not needing to move the feet prior to the strike making contact) This in no way means that the Alber cannot be used as an initial entry guard as stepping deep onto your opponent's second True Time can crowd them and give you the opportunity to apply other techniques.

Ringeck's additional guards

Ringeck makes reference to two additional guards in his Fechtbuch which are technically accounted for within the existing four guard positions, though the intention behind them is slightly different. In both cases Ringeck makes the statement: "...if you approach your opponent..." suggesting that it is a means by which to gain entry into the second True Time, and this does indeed seem to be the case although, unlike the Zornort, these are passive entry tactics, a method of drawing your opponent out by baiting him. By being in the extended position, you are placing your head, hands and sword in the outer periphery of the second True Time, whilst maintaining the body in the third, in much the same way as the Alber, making any threat given easy to control and quick to perform, as the counter-movement will be in Single Time.

The Langort

Now note what is called the Langort.
Take note: if you approach your opponent, place your left foot forwards and aim your point stretched out at his face or chest with extended arms. If he then strikes from above at your head, you should wind your sword against his blow and thrust at his face. Or if he strikes from above or from below at your sword, with the intention of striking your point aside, you should change through and thrust into the opening on his other side. Or if he strikes your sword strongly with his blow, let your sword move swiftly round; in this way you will strike him in the head. If he runs in towards you, you may use wrestling or cutting .
Be careful that it does not deceive you!

Expansion:
The Langort, or 'Longpoint', can be construed as representing an extension from the cross Ochs, and the stance of the Langort is similar to that of the Vom Tage second position, with the weight upon the forward foot. The position of the Langort is such that you present a static obstruction in the form of a threat with the point to your opponent's face. In order for your opponent to enter into

The position of the Langort

a strike, he first has to remove this threat which automatically puts you into a Single Time counter. The Langort can be taken with either foot forward, but be aware that, to have the same foot forward as the hand upon the foregrip, you will need to have your hands well into the second True Time, so this variation should only be used in earnest by an experienced fencer. In this example, we shall assume that you are a right-handed fencer.

To take the position of Langort, you will have your right hand on the foregrip of the sword and the left foot forward. Stand with your heels upon the centreline and feet a good stride's width apart, the forward foot pointing towards your opponent along the centreline and the back foot perpendicular to it, pointing outward. The rear leg should be nearly straight, the forward leg bent with the weight forward and the balance and reach being controlled by the forward leg. The left side of the body should be bladed towards your opponent and a straight line formed between the rear shoulder, hip and foot, though remember not to extend the forward shoulder beyond the forward knee. Your pommel hand should be in line with the forward shoulder with the upper arm horizontal, perpendicular to the centreline, and the forearm vertically upward, keeping the elbow tucked back. Your forehand should reach forward, inside the pommel arm, to take the foregrip position, extending the point directly at your opponent's face along the eye-line. As with the cross Ochs, the sword weight must be supported by the pommel hand and any manoeuvring performed with the forehand. This is the Langort as taken with the left foot forward by a right-handed fencer. For a left-handed fencer to take the Langort, the right foot must be forward, the left hand on the foregrip and the position above mirrored.

As mentioned previously, this guard can also be taken with the opposite foot forward, so for a right-handed fencer that is with the right foot forward and the right hand upon the foregrip. Stand with your heels upon the centreline and feet a good stride's width apart, the forward foot pointing towards your opponent along the centreline and the back foot perpendicular to it, pointing outward. The rear leg should be nearly straight, forward leg bent, with the weight forward and the balance and reach being controlled by the forward leg. The right side of the body should be bladed towards your opponent and a straight line formed between the rear shoulder, hip and foot, though remember not to extend the forward shoulder beyond the forward knee. Holding the sword above the shoulder line, with the blade pointing towards your opponent's face and along his eye-line, extend the hands in front of the forward shoulder as far as is comfortable, whilst still allowing the elbows to be flexed. Remember you are out of distance and this is a static, almost antagonistic, position before contact is made, so the rule concerning not extending the hands beyond the forward shoulder does not yet apply. Any action/reaction from this position will involve the straightening of the arms and the squaring of the shoulders, which is when this rule applies. For a left-handed fencer to take this position, the left hand must be on the foregrip and the left foot forward, mirroring and stance above.

Striking from Langort

As Ringeck states, should your opponent attempt to strike you upon the head, then engage and Wind against his blade, thrusting into the face or an upper opening. The Langort is a weak but versatile position, so should your opponent attempt idly to displace your blade, then you must not try to resist against the displacement but nimbly move your blade around it and immediately bring the tip back to the eye-line, maintaining the threat to the face and thrusting forward, should the opportunity arise. If your opponent becomes sufficiently frustrated at not being able to move the tip away, or to engage with your extended target, he will most likely bat your blade aside with some vigour, giving you the opportunity to use his effort to your advantage. Do not resist the displacement, but redirect the transfer of momentum and cut quickly around to the other side, stepping in as you do so and striking him on the head, or any other available target. Should your opponent step inside your tip, then look to the **Schnitt** or enter into Ringen.

Langort Notes

The position of the Schranckhutt

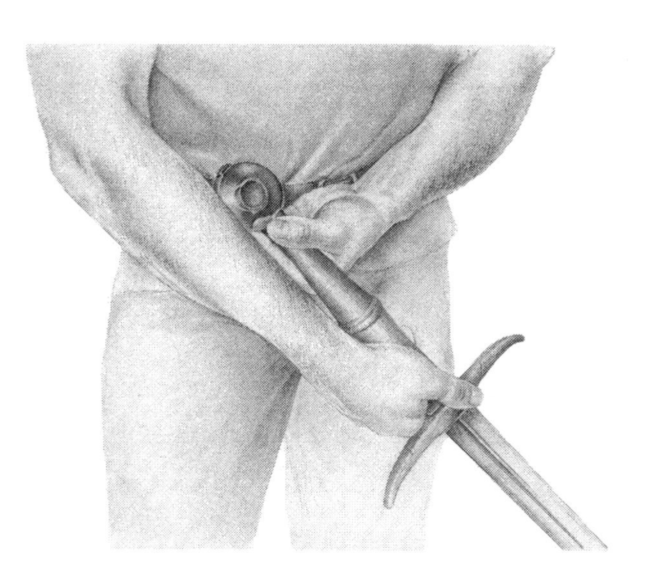

Right leg forward hand position

The Schranckhutt

The Schranckhutt is to be performed in this manner:
Item: if you approach your opponent, stand with your left foot forwards and place your sword with the point on the earth to your right side, with the long edge upwards, and from the left side the short edge should be below and the foot should be in front.

Expansion:
The Schranckhutt, or 'barrier guard', could be considered a derivative of the Alber though, when standing with your left foot forward, it is necessary to hold the sword in the false grip to overcome any weakness that the Alber would suffer in this position, hence "...point on the earth to your right side, with the long edge upwards...". However, this does make the position predominantly defensive rather than offensive and offers little more than an opportunity to cut into your opponent's blade with the intention of passing inside their tip and engaging him directly. But, as with the Langort and Alber, your hands are in the second True Time, making any action/reaction a Single Time movement, in this case most likely putting you in the Vor at the second intention as a consequence, rather than during the initial entry as with the Alber. The following examples assume that you are right-handed.

To take the position of the Schranckhutt, you will have your left foot forward and your right hand on the foregrip. Stand with your heels upon the centreline and your feet a good stride's width apart, the forward foot pointing towards your opponent along the centreline and the back foot perpendicular to it, pointing outward. The rear and forward leg should be bent with the weight slightly biased towards the front, the balance and reach being controlled by the forward leg. As with the Zornort, the hips should be approximately 45°, with the body leaning slightly forward and the shoulders square to your opponent, perpendicular to the centreline, a straight line being formed between the rear foot, hip and shoulder. With the arms strong and the hands in line with the waist, hold the sword above the centreline in the false grip, blade downward with the tip resting upon the ground to your right side. This is the position of the Schranckhutt from the right side, for the right-handed fencer. For the left-handed fencer, stand with your right foot forward, your left hand in the foregrip, and mirror the above stance.

The Schranckhutt, with your right foot forward and your right hand in the foregrip position, is as follows: Stand with your feet a stride's width apart, heels on the centreline, with the forward foot pointing towards your opponent and the back foot pointing outward, perpendicular to the centreline. Both your rear and forward leg should be bent, weight slightly forward-biased and above the centreline, with balance and reach being controlled by the front leg. The hips should be approximately 45° to the centreline with the shoulders as close to square with your opponent as is comfortable, the back being straight and the head forward with a straight line formed between the rear foot, hip and shoulder. Your forward arm, in this case the right, is slightly bent and laying across the thigh of the forward leg with your forehand on your left side. You should be gripping the handle in the false grip but with the palm on the forehand upward, thumb towards your opponent, and the sword handle resting along the inside of the forward forearm, thus keeping the forward wrist from twisting into a weak position. The pommel should be into the forward hip in line with the knee, and the pommel hand should have a secure, though light, grip and be easily-shifted within the hand. The short edge will be downward and the forward foot in front of the hands, the blade being just behind the line of the foot and close to perpendicular with the centreline, the point resting on the floor. This is the position for the Schranckhutt from the left side with the right foot forward. For a left-handed fencer, stand with your left foot forward, left hand on the foregrip, and mirror the above stance.

The entry from the Schranckhutt is simple; you will be looking to cut across your opponent with your first intention, passing through with the back foot towards your **open side** and looking to perform one of the Maisterhaw with your second intention. It is not impossible for you to strike your opponent from the first entry, but the likelihood of him being close enough for this to occur, without first presenting a threat to your **closed side**, is small. You are more likely to strike against the extended target of your opponent, as with the Alber, or directly against his blade to displace the threat away and enable you to enter into the Vor.

Striking from Schranckhutt

Standing in the Schranckhutt, if you sense a threat towards your closed side, then look to strike to your opponent's extended target as it comes into range by projecting the point towards his hands, turning the shoulders, hips and passing through with the back foot towards your open side, close to the centreline, as you do so. Be aware that, as a consequence of cutting into and not behind the strike of your opponent, you will find it difficult to reach the extended target before his strike becomes a threat.

If he is foolish enough to have passed through into distance with the back foot before his strike is completed, then he will be in the second True Time and sufficiently close for you to threaten him directly with an Oberhaw in your first intention. If your opponent is not so foolish, then you must look to cut against the flat of his blade with yours, so when you sense a threat towards your closed side you must start lifting your hands towards the threat. You should be looking to catch your opponent's strike within the Störck of your blade, drawing it into your crossguard as the shoulders and hips turn in towards your opponent, converting the defensive move into one of the Maisterhaw as the back foot passes through towards your open side to become the front foot of your new centreline, and completing the Maisterhaw as the now back foot moves to claim your new centreline position. Depending on whether your opponent is striking with the foot, or in the high or low line, dictates which of the Maisterhaw you will be converting your initial entry into. If he leads his strike with the foot and offers the extended target in your first intention then you look to the Krumphaw. If your opponent leads properly, with the hands, and threatens you with a strike into your upper quarter, then, with your second intention, strike a Zwerhaw towards his head. If he threatens you with a strike into your lower quarter then counter with a Schilhaw and strike/thrust towards their upper quarter.

Schranckhutt Notes

The Four Openings

Concerning the four openings.
Know the four openings: aim [well]; in this way you will strike surely without danger, without a doubt, regardless of how he acts.

Gloss.
In this lesson you are to recognise the four openings your opponent presents, to which you should always aim your fight. The first opening is the right side, the second is the left side above the opponent's belt. The other two openings are again on the right and left sides, but below the belt. Take heed of these openings so that you can fence in them. Aim skilfully without danger at whichever of the openings your opponent exposes, using a thrust with the long point, using **Nachraisen** and any other attacks. Pay no attention to how he bears himself towards you. In this way you will fight with certainty and will strike blows that hit, and by doing so you will prevent your adversary from achieving his attacks.

Expansion
Here we see the explanation of the four openings. The text explains how to identify the four openings and they are as such: Your opponent is facing you with his shoulders perpendicular to the centreline. Imagine a cross, the vertical component rising from the centreline and dissecting the body into a left and right side, the horizontal component crossing at the bottom of the rib cage and dissecting the body into an upper and lower half. You are now presented with four quarters: Upper left, upper right, lower left and lower right. Each quarter represents one of the four openings and where you must aim your fight with certainty and conviction, so preventing your opponent from presenting a counter.

The Four Versetzen

These are the four Versetzen, that injure or break the four guards.
Four are the Versetzen, that injure the [four] guards. Protect yourself from the Versetzen; if it happens it will greatly distress you.

Gloss.
Note: you have previously heard that you should fight only with four guards. You should also know the four Versetzen. These are four blows.
The first blow is the Krumphaw: it breaks the guard of Ochs.
The second is the Zwerhaw: it breaks the guard of Vom Tage.
The third is the Schilhaw: it breaks the guard of Pflug.
The fourth is the Schaytler: it breaks the guard [of] Alber.
And guard yourself against all Versetzen, which are used by bad fencers. Note too, when your opponent strikes you should strike as well, and when your opponent thrusts you should also thrust. You will find how to strike and thrust in the five blows and the Absetzen.

Expansion:
This is a vital key and explains why I made an earlier reference to the Maisterhaw being the back-bone of the system. The movements of the Maisterhaw, and the principles behind them, will provide you with every possible solution to entering into distance safely and all the subsequent techniques stem directly from them. Ringeck tells us that the four Versetzen are four of the Maisterhaw, excluding the Zornhaw as this is the entry into the first Nachraisen and does not set aside a blow so is not a Versetzen.

The four Versetzen break the four guards and Ringeck has enlightened us as to the following:

Krumphaw breaks the guard of Ochs
Zwerhaw breaks the guard of Vom Tage
Schilhaw breaks the guard of Pflug
Schaytler breaks the guard of Alber

Both Liechtenauer and Ringeck also make reference to the Versetzen used against you, Ringeck specifically commenting on those used by bad fencers. You could assume that he considers any Versetzen other than those within the Maisterhaw are bad, but as the Maisterhaw cover every possible variation of Versetzen you are likely to use, we can only surmise that he is referring to the ignorance of bad fencers generally. Part of the Art is about predicting the action of your opponent, but if your opponent has no knowledge or training in his action then there is no education within his reasoning, so making a reaction totally unpredictable. It is often the case that a bad fencer has no appreciation of danger and is unlikely to recognise when he is about to be killed, so he may not react in a predictable manner. This makes him dangerous not only to you but also to himself and it is often the case that an experienced fencer is humiliated by a beginner purely because the former is trying not to kill the latter.

Addition:
Important to principle
The four hand positions:
Upper or lower, left or right
These are the four quarters from which you must fight
The four openings are different from those of the guard
The position of the hands shows which entry is barred
As the guards are theirs and the entry is yours
The Maisterhaw will help you uncover their flaws.

Taking into consideration the numerous alternative positions that could be considered a guard, it is important for us to establish some rules by which to identify these numerous possibilities with respect to Liechtenauer's four guard positions, as described by Ringeck. Experience can offer great insight into the strengths and weaknesses of any static guard position and allow the individual to assume a guard and enter with a Versetzen appropriate to that position. However, for the less experienced student it is necessary to provide some general reference points, in order for him to make an educated guess and not be left in a vulnerable position.

When analysing the four guards we can deduce that each position takes advantage of one or more of the four openings, providing a first intention entry threat with a strike, a thrust, or both. The Vom Tage threatens a strike from above, the Alber a strike or thrust from below, the Ochs a thrust in the upper line and the Pflug a strike or thrust into the lower line. Now we must establish what it is about these guards that give them this threat in the first intention. It is safe to assume that any position where the point is towards the opponent will have a narrow line of entry and most likely be converted into a thrust, and any position where the point is away from the opponent will have a wide line of entry and most likely result in a strike. To enter with a strike in the highline will most likely result in an Oberhaw, but with a thrust this could be in either the high or low line, originating from above. To enter with a strike in the low line would generally result in an Underhaw, but a thrust could be in either the high or low line, originating from below.

We still have a significant number of variables to consider, so is there any simpler rule we can apply in order to know which Maisterhaw to use against a non-specific guard? Taking the view that the sword itself is not our concern, but more the person holding it, we can extrapolate a general rule from applying this same analysis to body mechanics as to the sword. Let us consider what it is that controls the weapon; the hands, the shoulder, the hips and then the feet. Analysing each individual element, the foot orientation is the slowest part to change and is fixed at the point of assuming a guard, so indicating which side the strike will originate from in the first intention from the third True Time is straightforward. If the left foot is forward, we can safely assume that the threat comes from their right side, and vice versa (though there are exceptions). Although moving faster, the direction of movement of the hips and shoulders is dictated by the feet, making these predictable also, thus leaving the hands as the only variable relative to the foot position. The four guards assume four separate hand positions relative to the geometry of the individual's body. Where the quarters of the four openings are upper and lower, left and right, relative to a reference perpendicular to the centreline, the four hand positions are in line with the centreline and very much dependent upon the orientation of the individual holding the sword. Like the four openings, the upper and lower line of the four hand positions is dictated by the bottom of the ribcage, but the vertical line passes just behind the forward shoulder and called forward and rearward, so depending on which foot is forward dictates which is the forward shoulder. The guard positions are depicted by where the forehand is relative to one of these four quarters and the hand positions relate to the guards and their respective type of entry, as follows:

Upper forward quarter –	Ochs, narrow line of entry from the upper line
Lower forward quarter –	Alber, wide line of entry from the lower line, conversion into a thrust is not impossible
Upper rearward quarter –	Vom Tage, wide line of entry, most likely downward, from the upper line
Lower rearward quarter –	Pflug, narrow line of entry from the lower line

Now you have a simple reference point for the four Versetzen relative to the foot orientation and hand position of the opponent's guard. By entering through the Zornort, with the intention of striking a Zornhaw, any of the four Versetzen is available to accommodate the action of your opponent, but having a point of reference from which to apply the Versetzen is useful for the beginner. If you have a good understanding of the Maisterhaw then it shouldn't matter how an opponent stands as each Maisterhaw is available to you at any time.

End of Addition

Overall Conclusion

We must conclude that the four guards, as recommended by Liechtenauer, provide us with every possible opportunity to cover one of the four openings and each guard must have advantages and disadvantages over that of the others. The following table allows us to reflect on this by grading each Versetzen relative to its effectiveness at breaking each guard position. The Langort and Schranckhutt are considered separately as they are already accommodated within Liechtenauer's 'The Four Guards'. First of all we must set the parameters of how we interpret each element within the table.

Taking the previous assessment of the guard positions we have established which attributes we associate with which guard.

Ochs: narrow line of entry from the upper line

Pflug: narrow line of entry from the lower line

Vom Tage: wide line of entry, most likely downward, from the upper line

Alber: wide line of entry from the lower line, conversion into a thrust is not impossible

The Versetzen are versatile, within their respective strengths and weaknesses, but also limited in the way they can be applied. If we briefly look at the Single Time movement possible from each one in turn, we can further analyse their effectiveness.

Krumphaw: a 'moving the centreline' entry with the intention of removing a thrust or strike from the high line, and strike from the low line, by displacing the opponent's target (you) whilst maintaining and controlling his threat upon its original centreline. Ideal for gaining the Vor in the second intention from the second True Time

Schilhaw: a 'claiming the centreline' entry with the intention of directly countering a thrust or strike from and to the low line by displacement with your sword, maintaining the original centreline and destabilising the opponent. Ideal for gaining the Vor in the second intention at the first True Time

Zwerhaw: a 'moving the centreline' entry with the intention of controlling a downward strike from the high line by displacing the opponent's target (you) whilst collecting and controlling his threat upon its original centreline, presenting a direct counter-threat in the high line into an upper quarter. Ideal for gaining the Vor in the second intention at the first True Time.

Schaytler: a 'claiming the centreline' entry with the intention of breaking a static threat from the low line by making a direct counter with the first intention into the high line. This is achieved by forcing your opponent from his position of advantage into one of defence, or at least counter, in order that he presents an opportunity for a Schilhaw in the first True Time or a Krumphaw in the second True Time. Ideal for breaking your opponent's Vor into the second True Time.

The gradings given within the table reflect the effectiveness of each Maisterhaw at breaking the relative guard positions and in relation to the above analysis:

intended - the Maisterhaw most suited to the characteristics of that guard

optional - a possible alternative to the intended Maisterhaw but not necessarily ideal, depending on how the guard breaks and the entry likely from it

unlikely - an improbable use of the Maisterhaw relative to the guard and the nature of an entry likely from it

flawed - totally inappropriate use of the Maisterhaw relative to the guard and the entry likely from it

Strike / *Guard*	Krumphaw	Schilhaw	Zwerhaw	Schaytler
Vom Tage	optional	unlikely	intended	flawed
Ochs	intended	flawed	optional	unlikely
Pflug	unlikely	intended	flawed	optional
Alber	unlikely	optional	flawed	intended
Langort	intended	flawed	optional	unlikely
Schrankhutt	unlikely	optional	flawed	intended

So we now have a simple reference of Versetzen with respect to guard position and can refine further our understanding of the importance of the Maisterhaw within the system. All of the Maisterhaw should become second nature and it isn't until this occurs that you can concentrate on developing the other skills necessary to progress further. There are 3 stages involved in learning the Art and each one is a natural progression towards the next, overlapping as an improvement in one leads into a better understanding of the rest.

The first stage is to understand yourself, how you move, where your weaknesses are and how to overcome them to your advantage. This is the foundation of your understanding and cannot be hurried or avoided. There will be those students who spend all their time understanding this stage and they may appear never to progress, but do not be impatient as a greater depth of knowledge regarding your own strengths and weaknesses creates a stronger foundation from which to build.

The second stage is to understand your opponent and this can only be achieved with experience. The more time invested in practising with a training partner, the greater the understanding of him. However, do not limit yourself, train with many different people, starting with those you know and trust and venturing into the unknown as your experience grows. NEVER put yourself in danger. If you do not trust an opponent, do not fence against him until you are ready.

The third and final stage is understanding yourself relative to your opponent and this is the last lesson to learn and, as with stages 1 and 2, a lesson that never ends. Again, only time and experience can provide you with this and it isn't until you understand the previous stages to a competent degree that you can even consider the third. This is the tactical application of what you understand about yourself relative to what you can glean from your opponent and where the expression of the Art truly begins.

Do not be impatient to learn and be prepared for the boredom of repetition before your Art develops. How you learn the Art is your own personal journey and how you apply that Art is an expression of yourself. No two fencers are the same in the way that no two people are the same. You may fence against different abilities, styles and disciplines but when you have reached a stage of competence, where you no longer need to consider what you know as a system, all Arts become the same and the art of fence takes a different persona. Good luck in your journey!

What we have covered:

Grade 1

(A minimum of 3 hours training a week for 3 months)

A basic understanding of the fundamental components of the system

Step A

- Recognise and name the 4 guards as well as the Schranckhutt, Langort and Zornhort, and also the 5 Maisterhaw and their relationship towards one another
- Recognise and name the anatomy and characteristics of the sword
- Recognise and name the 4 openings and the four hand positions relative to their guards
- Explain the proper way of striking and the striking sequence

Step B *(demonstrating includes showing an understanding and explaining)*

- Demonstrate the strikes and the guards proficiently
- Demonstrate the use of the different parts of the sword (including the Schwech, Störck. long edge, short edge, pommel and crossguard, percussive and perceptive nodes and the rotational points)

- Break the 4 static guards with a compliant partner

Step C

- Breaking a static guard with opposition
- Entering with the Zornort and the proper way of striking

Grade 2

(A minimum of 5 months, or equivalent attendance, after achieving Grade 1)

Grade 1 in a dynamic environment to demonstrate proper body co-ordination, balanced movement and correct posture. Using the Zornhaw as defence

Step A

- Recognise and understand the four True Times in relation to striking and distance

Step B *(demonstrating includes showing and teaching using shinai simulators)*

- Teach the entirety of Grade 1 to a beginner
- Demonstrate the True Time using a dynamic guard change (moving from one guard to another) and a guard change with a strike (using a strike to move from one guard to another), all against a compliant partner
- Enter using the half-step and use the Zornhaw to counter an attack and either strike your partner, end up in an advantageous position or finish in the bind

Step C

- As in step B, but against a non-compliant partner (i.e. the partner moves between guards with an offensive manoeuvre, returning to a guard of his choosing without informing the student graduating)

Next...

In Grade 3 we will further expand on the Nachraisen, the Fühlen and the In Des, and cover the theory and application of the Eussere, Überlauffen, Zucken, Durch wechseln, Abnemen, Feler, Verkerer and the three pieces from the Zornhaw, introducing the concept of Winden as a consequence.

Glossary of Terms

Alber low line forward guard (see 'The Four Guards)

bind static contact between two blades, usually in the low line

centreline an imaginary straight line passing through your heels, and at the beginning and end of a movement it should always be towards the centre of your opponent, representing the shortest distance between you both, the orientation for the individual being dictated by where the heels are aligned

closed side the side from which it is difficult to defend in Single Time without passing through with the back foot, e.g. if the left foot is forward then the left side is closed

Durch wechseln changing through from one side of your opponent's blade to the other

Ersetzen setting aside the blade of your opponent with your own

Fectbuch fight book

first intention the movement concerning the initial entry into the first True Time

forehand the forward hand, or the hand upon the foregrip, e.g. for a right-handed fencer the forehand will be the right hand, and vice versa

foregrip the position on the grip where the forehand is placed, close to the crossguard

Fühlen the sense of feeling concerning your opponent's strength and intention when in the bind

half-step a step with the forward foot

halfsword holding the sword with the forehand on the foregrip, the pommel hand holding the blade about the centre

hammer strike a strike performed by holding the sword with both hands upon the blade and striking using a hammering action with the intent of hitting with the crossguard and/or pommel

HEMA Historical European Martial Arts

high line above the line of the waist

In des simultaneity or without hesitation

inside see **'open side'**

Krone a defensive movement that requires the crossguard to be raised in front of the face and above the head with the blade pointing upward, usually to displace a thrust to the face

Krumphaw strike to the extended target (see 'The Maisterhaw')

Langort an extension from the Ochs (see 'Ringeck's Additional Guards')

low line below the line of the waist

lower line see **'low line'**

Maisterhaw master strikes

Messer large, single-edged weapon, not too dissimilar to a modern machete

Nach after, or 'chase'

Nachraisen travelling after, an important principle covered in Grade 3

Oberhaw a downward strike

Ochs highline forward guard (see 'The Four Guards')

open side the side from which you are likely to defend in Single Time, dictated by the forward foot, e.g. if the left foot is forward then the right side is open

outside see **'closed side'**

pass back a step with the forward foot going back to become the back foot

pein a process by which a bar or rod, extruding from an insecure object, is hammered over in order to enlarge the end and form a rivet like protrusion, thus firmly sandwiching the object and making it secure, specifically in the case of a pommel being secured onto a tapered tang

Pflug low line rear guard (see 'The Four Guards')

Ringen wrestling

Schaytler strike used against the Alber (see 'The Maisterhaw')

Schilhaw strike used against a threat into the lower quarter (see 'The Maistehau')

Schnitt a method of cutting achieved by placing the sharp edge of the blade upon the target and pushing against or pulling through in order to achieve the cut, much like carving meat

Schranckhutt forward defensive position taken in the low line (see 'Ringeck's Additional Guards')

second intention the second movement after the initial entry into the first True Time, the initial entry being the first intention

Single Time a movement with the hands, thus without the need to include the body or foot/feet

Störck the part of the blade from the crossguard to the centre of its length

Schwech the part of the blade from the centre of its length to the tip

Underhaw an upward strike

upper line see **'high line'**

Versetzen a displacement of a threat with your blade

Vom Tage high line rear guard (see 'The Four Guards')

Vor before, or 'lead'

Wechsel change

Winden winding, or a dynamic displacement performed against an opponent's sword, usually resulting in a thrust to one of the four openings

Zornhaw an aggressive strike along the centreline (see 'The Maisterhaw')

Zornort a transitional entry position along the centreline and forward, coming from the low line (see 'The Maisterhaw')

Zwerhaw a strike against an Oberhaw in the high line (see 'The Maisterhaw')

Notes

Notes

Notes

Notes

Notes

Notes

Notes

Printed in Great Britain
by Amazon